A SCIENTIFIC LOOK AT THE CONCEPTS OF SOUL, REBIRTH, WORK AND THE LAW OF KARMA
An Attempted Synthesis

A SCIENTIFIC LOOK AT THE CONCEPTS OF SOUL, REBIRTH, WORK AND THE LAW OF KARMA
An Attempted Synthesis

ANIL VISHNU MOHARIR

ZORBA BOOKS

ZORBA BOOKS

Publishing Services by Zorba Books, 2019

Website: www.zorbabooks.com
Email: info@zorbabooks.com
Copyright © **Anil Vishnu Moharir**

Revised, enlarged and updated edition 2019
A Scientific Look at the Concepts of Soul, Rebirth,
Work and the Law of Karma : An Attempted Synthesis

ISBN Print Book - 978-93-88497-84-8
ISBN eBook - 978-93-88497-85-5
Second edition

First Published: 2017, Zorba Books, Gurugram, Haryana, India
ISBN 978-93-5265-930-2

All rights reserved. No part of this book may be reproduced or transmitted in any form or by any means, electronic or mechanical, except by a reviewer. The reviewer may quote brief passages, , with attribution, in a review to be printed in a magazine, newspaper, or on the Web—without permission in writing from the copyright owner.

The publisher under the guidance and direction of the author has published the contents in this book, and the publisher takes no responsibility for the contents, it's accuracy, completeness, any inconsistencies, or the statements made. The contents of the book do not reflect the opinion of the publisher or the editor. The publisher and editor shall not be liable for any errors, omissions, or the reliability of the contents of the book.

Any perceived slight against any person/s, place or organization is purely unintentional.

Zorba Books Pvt. Ltd.(opc)
Gurgaon, INDIA

To
SIYA AND SAMARTH ISHAN
My loving grand-daughter and grand-son

CONTENTS

Foreword to the first edition
by Professor Dr. Ravin Lakshman Thatte.......................... xi
Foreword to the second edition
by Swami Suparnanand Maharaj xvii
Preface to the first edition
by Professor Dr. Anil Vishnu Moharir xix
Preface to the second edition by Dr. Anil Vishnu Moharir xxvii
Front-piece to the book- LORD DATTATREYA xxxi

CHAPTER-1 : A Scientific Look at the Concept of 'Soul' 1

1.1 Abstract 1
1.2 Introduction and background information 3
1.3 Necessity of scientific theory for life after death/reincarnation 8
1.4 Dawn of the scientific and industrial revolution and implications 15
1.5 Everything in the universe is made of atoms: Recycling is the fundamental law of nature 17
1.6 Observed and reported cases of reincarnation/rebirth/life after death 26
1.7 Vedic philosophy about birth, death and reincarnation/rebirth 29
1.8 Religious philosophies are based on third-person accounts 31
1.9 Modern concept of atoms and molecules: Their structures, combinations and functions 32
1.10 Quanta and quantum particles 35
1.11 What is Life? 37
1.12 What is Soul? 46
1.13 Kundalini and human consciousness 51

1.14 Evidence for the existence of nadis and chakras 54
1.15 What is death? and how does it come about? 55
1.16 Mind as a dynamic responsive attribute and also a reflection of the body interacting with continually changing fluxes of universal energy 59
1.17 Vedic view of the structure and composition of the soul : The Panch-kosh Siddhanta 61

CHAPTER 2 : Questions about Soul and Rebirth: Need for a fresh look and redefinition 67

2.1 Abstract 67
2.2 Introduction 69
2.3 A case of factual reality and redefining rebirth 71
2.4 Possible role of synthesized proteins in controlling behavior, actions and in state of enlightenment 72
2.5 Religious philosophies are based on third-person accounts / meta-narrative books 74
2.6 Our criteria for considering and accepting rebirth 77
2.7 Everything in the universe is made of atoms 79
2.8 Need for new thinking and explanation on our traditional concepts 81

CHAPTER 3: Work, Its Origin, Kinds and the Law of Karma: A Synthesis for their Scientific Foundation and Human Obligations. 88

3.1 Abstract 88
3.2 Why there is perpetual work in nature? 89
3.3 Merging boundaries of Physics, Physical Chemistry and Biochemistry of matter 95
3.4 Work, nature of work and Classification of work 96
3.5 New Science of Epigenetics 99
3.6 The mechanism of DNA methylation 101
3.7 Epigenetics in relation to the inherited and accumulated work (Karma) 103
3.8 Pure and impure work 105

3.9 The process of accumulating work, the 'sanchit-karma', the Concept of the Mythological character 'Chitragupta' who writes down the details of our good and bad karma done from birth to death and human obligations 107
3.10 Natural delineation of work, their signals and responsibility of parents..110
3.11 Interdependence for work in societies and the division of labour 111
3.12 Ethical and moral obligation in the performance of work..113
3.13 Obligations, responsibilities and conduct for Scientists 114

References... 116
Abstract on the first edition of the book published in 2017 with views and comments received from readers.......124-127
Note on the contribution of Dr. Anil Vishnu Moharir to science.... 134

FOREWORD TO THE FIRST EDITION

Ever since Georges Lemaitre (1894-1966), Belgian Astronomer and Cosmologist observed that all heavenly bodies (stars and galaxies) are moving away from each other at very high speed, inferring thereby that the universe probably had its origin in a cataclysmic explosion of a small primeval 'body' all recent experimental evidence has pointed in the same direction. This observation now goes by the popular term 'the big bang' first proposed somewhat derisively by the British Astronomer and Astrophysicist Sir Fred Hoyle, the proponent of the 'steady-state theory of universe' which holds that our universe did not get created but is pristine and has always existed as it is. This work was done together with Jayant Narlikar an Indian astrophysicist. The changes, within this universe, may appear to be evolutionary in nature yet can be explained by the existing laws of physics. The Jains or the followers of Jainism in India also hold a similar point of view. The great Gautam Buddha seemed to have been reluctant to speculate as to how our universe could have come about and instead advised his followers to focus on the infirmities of this sensorial world. The Middle Eastern Abrahamic religions are too theistic to be included in this kind of discussion.

It is in one of the other branches of Indian philosophy, traditionally associated with Hinduism that we find references to theories on the origin of the universe. These speculations are diverse but each one of them takes for granted that the universe had a beginning from a single source. One such speculation states in a verse 'With heat the Brahma expands and what follow are matter, life, mind and man'. It also calls this progressively changing scenario as 'Karm'. The word Brahma given to this primal body implies a process of expansion because it comes from the Sanskrit root 'Brih' to mean to spread or to roar. The modern theories in astronomical / cosmological physics or cosmogenesis, appear to have a similar 'view point' in which the thing that expanded is called a singularity because nothing else existed at that time which has been calculated to be about fourteen billion years ago. Even in theoretical physics, the nature of this singular entity is admitted to be beyond comprehension at least in the foreseeable future. Language fails here because in the absence of space no movement is possible; and therefore, a verb cannot be used; because it is single, comparisons are not feasible and therefore adjectives cannot be used; and being single, to give it a name becomes superfluous. 'That thing' if it can be called as such is speculated to be in a state of utter or absolute equivalence in terms of forces, if any, within it. How and why this equivalence gets to be tweaked leading to the events that follow is likely to remain a mystery in the foreseeable future but the nature of the violent and extremely hot events that followed this change are now somewhat within the grasp of human understanding.

As the details get worked out one thing must remain uncontested that the singularity or Bramh is our forbearer. Forefather would be a wrong word because the evolution of gender is a very recent event in comparison to the estimated figure of fourteen billion years ago when the singularity or Bramh exploded and subsequently began to expand. In what is probably an all-time classic, Sant Dnyaneshwar (1275-1296 AD) a philosopher extraordinaire from Maharashtra, while narrating a commentary on Shrimad Bhagwad Geeta in his very first verse uses the word-Atmaroopa to describe this basic singularity. The word is in two parts; Atma to mean force and Roopa to mean form. This is as good a definition or description of the singularity, as you can get because it encapsulates the sequence of events that followed the 'big bang'. The forms that are inherited from this singularity must carry in them the forces that occupied the singularity till such a time that they last or speculatively get rolled back into the singularity after the original force that caused the expansion wanes and when gravitational forces take over and the universe collapses or rolls back on itself as happens to many a star during their life time in this universe.

At a fundamental level what we call as the inanimate universe ticks on due to a play of energy and it is this energy that at some point comes to express itself as living matter albeit only in a few molecules but this transformation has enormous implications. As living matter evolves and becomes more complex, the energy or force within living cells comes to evolve towards more sophisticated forms and perform an array of functions. Modern physics beginning with Einstein have described matter and energy as two faces of the same coin in that in an atom, its constituents such as electrons, manifest and disappear leaving behind a trail which can only be experienced 'post-facto' and then regenerate again as a particle. This trail is viewed as electrical in nature for want of a better word. In living organisms where a complicated array of atoms, molecules and compounds work in tandem during life, the routes that get established to keep the systems going are called 'ion channels' because it is the ionic form of the atom which is responsible for the end use and the consequent result. This extraordinary play is possible because it is codified in the genome which virtually acts as a choreographer to sustain life. The genome is vulnerable to change by atmospheric radiation, sensitive as it is, and though it may undergo a change it continues to sustain itself as a reproductive unit ushering in changes both in function and structure in its new AVATAR. That word AVATAR means incarnation or re-incarnation, hinting subtly that the same clay which in fact is in a 'modified energy state' is now manifesting in a different form.

The word MAYA frequently used by Indian philosophers needs to be explained here. That word in fact means the creative potential of Bramh or the singularity. The observable universe or the nature at large as we see it, is a part of this creative impulse and according to some philosophers is as real as the singularity while some other philosophers believe that only the Bramh is the absolute truth relegating the manifested world to a somewhat inferior position calling it a 'relative truth'.

Dr. Anil Moharir, a physicist with vast experience in agricultural research was in a unique position to observe nature in all its splendour but also uniquely he did not stop at the feeling of the wonder that resulted in his mind by his observations. He has not only delved deep into the literature on the subject of botany and plantology but in addition has delved in physics which by a common agreement is now considered to be the fountainhead of all matters scientific. He therefore reaches back across huge swathes of time to espouse the idea of unity (or the soul) of this variegated universe, and yet, allows within his arguments the 'energy based mechanization ' of both the non- living as well as the living matter. In the mind of this reviewer, Dr. Moharir might be introducing an entirely new branch of philosophy to the existing schools. In this small book, Dr. Moharir has proposed four new premises and logically discussed them in the light of modern theories and the Standard Model of Elementary Particle Physics; they are (1) the hitherto enigmatic 'soul' is nothing else but the *de facto primal* electric charge, (2) souls of all living organisms remain in continual connection with each other from their birth to death with this universal electric energy continuum, or cosmic consciousness (3) rebirth / reincarnation of individual souls as is popularly believed is scientifically impossible and continues to be a popular myth. (4) rebirth / reincarnation merely represents the birth of a new individual, resembling in it's characteristics with someone who had lived in the historical past arising out of the self-replicating behaviour of the DNA (*Deoxyribonucleic acid*) molecules in associated interaction with epigenetic environment which in fact is a modified version of the original electrical environment

The technical terminology that he employs is erudite yet is well within the scope of an average reader with a modicum of scientific background such as this reviewer and the way he marshals his facts is 'awesome' to use a popular modern expression. His view stretching the Indian intellectual tradition to nearly ten thousand years appeared to me far-fetched during the first reading of his book but recent excavations since then have unearthed some data which suggests that Dr.Moharir might be justified in his conclusions in this regard.

To sum up, this book is a *'tour de force'* and those who read it, are sure to have an enriching experience. I congratulate Dr. Anil Moharir on this painstaking task and showing enough courage to back his scientific intuition and also for presenting a holistic multidisciplinary overview of the complex and socio-culturally controversial subjects such as the 'Soul' and 'Rebirth'. This is a splendid effort. For me, it had been a great pleasure and also a rewarding experience to read this book.

Ravin Thatte

Prof. Dr. Ravin L. Thatte
MS, FRCS (Edin.), Ad Hominen
Plastic & Reconstructive Surgeon
46, Shirish Co-Op Hsg, Society
187, Veer Savarkar Marg,
Mumbai, Maharashtra, 400 016

THE RAMAKRISHNA MISSION INSTITUTE OF CULTURE
(A Branch Centre of Ramakrishna Mission, P.O. Belur Math, Dist. Howrah, West Bengal-711 202)
GOL PARK   KOLKATA - 700 029, WEST BENGAL, INDIA
Phone : 033-4030-1200, 2464-1303/04/05, 2466-1235/36/37
Fax: 033-2464-1307; E-Mail: golpark.rmic@rkmm.org, rmic.golpark@gmail.com, rmic.secretary@gmail.com; Website : www.sriramakrishna.org

August 5, 2019

Foreword

The Book entitled *'A Scientific Look at The Concepts of Soul, Rebirth, Work And The Law of Karma—An Attempted Synthesis'* By Dr. Anil Vishnu Moharir traces the development in efforts and difficulties encountered in understanding the concept of the Transmigration of Soul and its rebirth being discussed for over 5,000 years of human history. Readers will carefully note that the author argues against the old concept of 'Soul' taking its permanent residence within the body of an organism from the moment of birth to its death. It has, instead, been argued that the so called 'Soul' actually remains in continual connection with the universal consciousness from the moment of conception, development, birth to death through 'electric charge' mediated within millions of ion channels in bodies of living organisms. The Author claims that the book is not a narrative on metaphysical entities such as 'soul' or 'rebirth' but a multidisciplinary synthesis to assert what we have been assuming to be metaphysical for centuries in the past but actually a physical entity. The task of compiling a comprehensive multidisciplinary review article with a purely scientific outlook about such a complex subject as 'Soul' is a daunting task. It can have a value to the students of science and technology. But the old concept of soul or Spirit beyond mind and intellect is discussed at full length by the Yogis who seek it in their meditation. It is also experienced in Deep Sleep State. In deep sleep, we exist in Spirit(Atman) which is divine. That is why spirit is indescribable and is non-physical as well. Mind, intellect are all material elements. Atman alone is conscious.

The concept of Soul does not fall within the domain of Reason as it is beyond body, mind and intellect. Since Soul is not a material object, it cannot be understood by any physical means. The Kathopanisad says that it can be perceived by the pointed and subtle intellect only. What we call Manas, the mind, the Western people call soul. The West never had the idea of soul until they got it through Sanskrit Philosophy in 1870s. This is the view of Swami Vivekananda. Mind and intellect belong to the Sukshma Sarira, (Subtle body) made of fine particles like five sense organs (eyes, ears, nose, skin, tongue). This subtle body is the doer, enjoyer. Spirit/ Soul requires several births to perfect itself. The Soul takes up a new body after it gives up the old one. There is a definite law here, though very subtle. Soul, being deathless, leaves the old body and takes up a new one according to the Karma and Jnana (knowledge) it acquired in the previous births. Thus, the law of Karma assumes a pivotal role for the Soul to choose its next births. When Karma is purified, mind and Buddhi also become purified, gradually; spirit manifests itself to the Sadhaka in full glory. One may have question as to how it happens. The answer is in the Dream State experience of ours. In dream, mind separates itself from the body; body lies in the bedstead but mind moves out of body and creates a new world from nowhere and enjoys it, suffers from it. In dream, we may dream some such dream that enables us to see our own body lying on the bedstead. Sometimes, in rare occasions, we see our own body lying dead, as it were, and sitting around our dead body are weeping our relatives. This is the best of all dreams since we feel then that we are not body but we have a body each. Of course, when we enter the body our sleep is gone. When our minds re-enter our body after the dream, we go to live. But when we cannot do that, we die. We give up body; we are dead. This is the Law of Karma and transmigration of Soul in brief. In a roundabout way, Suddha Karma grants us freedom by making our mind Unselfish.

The book under reference is the revised and enlarged edition of Dr. Moharir's first version published in 2017. The new concepts he introduced in this second edition are elaborated as under:

i) Karma— its origin, its kind and its law, ii) Relating the law of Karma to the Big Bang and its aftermath, iii) Ancient concepts of Karma such as Prarabdha karma, Kriyaman Karma and Sanchita Karma etc.

He has also shown quite enthusiastically and interestingly the bonding between Chitragupta's Balance Sheet of Karma at the Celestial Office of the God of Death (Yamaraj) and the modern concept of DNA Mythylation.

The author can rightfully claim that he has made a most fascinating contribution to the old subject of Soul and its way to perfection. He has also presented a holistic overview of the much contested subjects of 'soul' and its rebirth guided by his chosen domain of scientific instincts. The book has already aroused intellectual curiosity among the scientists in particular and the intelligentsia in general.

May God bless the author!

(Swami Suparnananda)
Secretary

Swami Suparnanand Maharaj
Secretary & Chairman
Ramkrishna Missin Institute of Culture
Kolkata, West Bengal, India

PREFACE TO THE FIRST EDITION

The concepts of 'Soul' and 'Re-birth' have been associated with human psyche for millions of years and have become a part and parcel of our religious dogmatic faith for granted. Throughout history, all cultures have postulated the existence of a 'Soul'. A scientific field of the discipline known as 'Psychology' is supposed to study everything about what is called 'Soul'. Even so, psychologists in practice do not actually study soul, but only human behavior and more recently, the human brain. Still however, a substantial majority of human population from all over the world does not subscribe to the concept of soul for various reasons. Nor do they have logical reasons for explaining the continued existence and repeated emergence of the characteristics features and traits of all the living species on the earth in cycles of birth and death. Despite millions of years that have gone by in the history of existence on earth, man is still searching for his roots of origin and the force that drives him from birth to death. This book traces the developments in efforts and difficulties encountered in understanding the enigmatic concepts of 'Soul' and 'Re-birth' being discussed for over 10,000 years and yet being far away from a global consensus. The reasons are more of religious dogma, pride, divide, blind faith, false sense of superiority of one religion over other, and above all; fear and lack of courage on the part of people to cross the religious and social barriers arising out of the teachings, interpretations, beliefs and dogma of religious and 'meta-narrative' books to rebel in favour of purely scientific logic, reason and truth. The concepts of both 'Soul' and 'Re-birth' have been propagated and entrenched in the minds of people for thousands of years more by the religious preachers as part of their philosophies rather than on scientific merits. No surprise, despite tremendous developments in material sciences, elementary particle physics, space science and technology, genetics and molecular biology, our understanding of the concept of 'Soul', its meaning, universality, nature, constitution, structure, function and physical location within body in relation to cosmology, structure of matter, terrestrial environment, physiology, psychology, biochemistry, thought process, concept, nature of memory and physical behavior are still not known in a holistic way. The author argues against the old concept of 'Soul' taking its permanent residence within the body of an organism from the moment of birth to its death. It has instead been argued that the so called 'Soul' the *de-facto* electric charge, actually remains in continual connection on its own with the universal consciousness (electric potential continuum) from the moment of conception, gestation, development and birth and all through life to the last breath until death, by means of the 'electric charge' mediated through millions of ion channels within bodies of living organisms. In a way, it is the same universal electrical energy that mediates our localized individual creation, operation, motivation, sustenance, existence and finally destruction. Whenever the physical body of any living organism from the unicellular bacteria to the most evolved of all species the human being is incapacitated for the sustained flow of electric charge / universal consciousness / ionic movements within itself to drive electric currents through specific ion-channels in motivating the conscious body, death occurs. Death in any multi-cellular organism is therefore not an instantaneous process but a gradual withdrawal of electric flow as a result of progressive closing of ion-channels from various organs and parts in a sequential order. The Vedic concept and structural model for the Soul, described about 8,000 years BC, has been described, argued and logically discussed in relation to the modern developments in science and the known facts about life to assert that everything attributed to and described about the qualities and properties of the enigmatic 'Soul' are also factually true about the- 'Electric Charge'. Therefore, there is merit in assuming that under dogmatic influences of religious beliefs, descended down to us through hundreds of centuries, we have perhaps lost courage to review / introspect / argue / question our blind belief and have failed to recognize 'Electric Charge' to be the *de-facto* 'Soul' that indeed drives the entire universe and the living world on the earth, irrespective of its terrestrial, aquatic or plant origins. Still however, until a global consensus is built up on purely scientific (multidisciplinary) merits, the Vedic concept of 'Soul' stands tall and provides a logical, quasi-scientific explanation to satisfy the innate human curiosity about life and what drives the living world. Any discussion or explanation on 'Soul' is incomplete without such discussion on another enigmatic concept of 'Re-birth' and 'cycles of re-birth' and death. And I am obliged and compelled to include another comprehensive article with focus exclusively on the concept of 'Re-birth' as an independent chapter, even at the risk of some unavoidable repeatation. Here again it has been argued that there appears to be an incorrect interpretation on the whole concept of rebirth as first explicitly described in the Shrimad Bhagwad Geeta and descended down to us through thousands of years without question, introspection or applying independent mind. Modern science does not support rebirth of an individual from the past. At the same time, it provides ample scope, possibility, explanation and understanding of an individual being born today from interaction of the self-replicating DNA molecules assisted by epigenetic environmental conditions of growth with characteristics and properties of head, heart and valour, similar or nearly identical to someone who had lived in the historical past and memories about whom have been kept alive in our records or conscious memory through generations. This is because, in accepting rebirth of any individual from the past, we always compare similarities in such individual characteristics rather than their physical looks, body structure or constitution. And such replications of characteristic traits are being routinely done and expressed since millions of years by the self-replication of the DNA molecules.

The task of compiling a comprehensive multidisciplinary review article with a purely unbiased scientific outlook about such a complex subject as 'Soul' was a daunting task, particularly in view of extremely confusing viewpoints, perceptions, discussions and interpretations done by thousands of authors who have written volumes on these concepts. Again, millions of people have imbibed into their minds, innumerable variations of the descriptions of the concepts of Soul and Rebirth, acquired from equally diverse surroundings, social background and grooming in childhood. Today, it is very difficult to expect that all readers will have a uniformly common multi-disciplinary scientific training and socio-religious background, comprehension, perception and understanding besides willingness to welcome and consider radically different and unorthodox thoughts with courage and convictions. One of the reasons for my writing this book is to induce science oriented readers and particularly the scientists from any discipline to think in my way of understanding, logic and reasoning. Still, it is hoped that the readers would appreciate the efforts with an unbiased, unprejudiced mind and read something unconventional. Little efforts on their part to understand some of the most modern scientific phenomena and their relationships with the living world in understanding the concepts of 'Soul' and 'Re-birth' as described will facilitate comprehension of the subject matter of this small book.

This comprehensive review article is a revised, enlarged and updated version of the original presentation made by me under identical title at the 88th session of the Indian Philosophical Congress held at Sri Venkateshwara University, Tirupati, Andhra Pradesh, India, 17-19 th October, 2014. In the mean time, I had myself voluntarily subjected the pre-publication draft of this article for review and comments to several of my scientist colleagues, friends and well known authorities in this area of subject specialty and whereas most of them avoided to send any critical or non-critical comments or opinion, some just thanked me for the unnecessary thankless job I had undertaken. Still however, I do not personally feel so. Like any curious individual, born into a traditional Hindu family in India, concepts of soul and rebirth had been a passion with me and I indeed felt restless in not being able to grasp any clear comprehension about both these enigmatic concepts despite reading the best of books available on the subject from some of the most eminent scholars since my own childhood. A budding physicist within me and my inner curiosity never left me satisfied until I attempted to write myself on these subjects and on the present book. I have always believed that no concepts, ideas, beliefs or thoughts prevail in human civilazations for thousands of years without reason. But whenever, there arises any conflict, confusion or misinterpretations between concepts held dear to our hearts and the progress in contemporary science, it is the responsibility of the scientists to clear doubts and attempt to remove the misconceptions. The present book is only an honest attempt made in this direction. And in doing so, I do not claim that all that I have written may be the factual truth in reality, but in the absence of any clear direction, I have labored to look to our ancient concepts from the point of view of as many scientific disciplines as possible. It is merely an attempt on my part to join the missing scientific links and possibly build a complete picture that I could see. I am particularly grateful to Shri Sadh Guru Jaggi Vasudev, a renowned philosopher, speaker, writer and mystic Guru, for reading my original core-article and sending me his blessings and to Professor Vidya Bhushan Gupta, Retired Dean, Indian Institute of Technology, Delhi, a Polymer Physicist of international standing and currently a devoted follower in the order of 'Radha Saomi Satsang faith' from Dayal Bagh, Agra for appreciation, admiration and liking this article. I am also particularly grateful to Professor Dr. Ravin Thatte, MS, FRCS (Edin.), an internationally acknowledged researcher and plastic and reconstructive surgeon from Mumbai, and a multidisciplinary, multidimensional thinker, scholar and writer in his own right on the philosophy of 'Dnyaneshwari' and 'Geeta' for painstakingly going through each and every word of the manuscript and suggesting vital corrections and editorial changes. I am also grateful to Professor Rupert Sheldrake, a renowned biologist, writer, speaker and critic from England and originator of the concepts and theories of 'morphogenetic fields, morphic resonance and morphogenesis' for going through the manuscript and for magnanimously bringing out the fact in precise words and I quote "...that this article indeed contains so much in correlating together many different strands of thought with modern physiology and points to deeper interconnections within physics". This observation, coming from a biologist (with multidisciplinary background) of the stature of Professor Rupert Sheldrake is particularly satisfying, nay gratifying to me personally with a sense of fulfillment of a mission in life. Likewise, considerable appreciation received from Professor Dick Frans Swaab, Head of Department, Netherland Institute of Neuroscience, University of Amsterdam, Netherland and well known researcher on human brain has been encouraging. Endowed with a basic Masters degree in physics, later a Ph.D. in Fibre Science and Textile Technology and a practical work experience for over 37 years as a practicing transmission electron microscope specialist in agricultural research, I am amused to have emerged with a rare combination of capacity, experience with advantage for developing a broad inter- and multidisciplinary mental canvas. All that exists within dimensional limits from 10^{-14} to 10^{28} cm, incidentally the known expanse of our universe, interests me with a rare privilege to not only understand but to distinctly see and perceive the undercurrent of universal continuum of creation and connectivity through the artificial disciplinary boundaries. To explore and elucidate deep connections between different phenomena in nature is one of the most exciting and natural instincts of a trained physicist and I am no exception. And I have great desire and urge to not only know all this for myself but I have my intense desire to tell all about what I have explored to those who are anxious to know. It was therefore thought worthwhile to bring out this small publication with an allotted **ISBN** number for wider dissemination and discussion amongst scholars of oriental and scientific philosophy and to provoke the younger generation of scholars to critically look to the ancient concepts from purely scientific point of view. I shall not be surprised if they realize that the ancient 'Rishis' from India, who lived more than 10,000 years ago from now were certainly very close *(if not very precisely)* to the modern scientific understanding of nature and natural material creation. All we need to do today is to search, reveal, correlate and re-interpret the hard-core camouflaged science from the ancient texts with corresponding modern scientific terminologies.

Apparently, what is not rational, logical or scientifically relevant from the ancient texts needs to be filtered out and what is relevant, needs to be integrated into a continually evolving scientific thought. The task is not an easy one but certainly not impossible, if everyone (particularly scientists from related disciplines) attempts to develop the right kind of mindset and evolve himself / herself in a multi-disciplinary mode and understanding. This is just a beginning and I hope, that someone from amongst the readers may take the cue and explore such new concepts from ancient literature and provide them the necessary modern scientific foundation. I am aware, that in my attempt to write on such complex subjects as 'Soul' and 'Rebirth' from a multidisciplinary point of view, some words, terms, entities and theoretical concepts may appear to be cropping up abruptly in the description without any formal background and introduction to the reader. No wonder, it is not unlikely for some readers for want of a multidisciplinary background, they may appear to be speculative. My own convictions as a professional scientist is that if our theoretical foundations for reasoning are sound, conclusions on expected lines are speculatively in-built within. But this is unavoidable because each conceptual terminology would otherwise require at least a paragraph in explaining description. And considering limitations and scope of the present book, this was just not possible to do so. Therefore, I have provided the pertinent list of all the references, literature and books to which any curious reader may revert for in depth understanding. At best, I can only assure the readers of this book that I have intended and attempted to explore the scientific foundations behind our ancient concepts of soul and rebirth to the best of my ability, comprehension and capability of interpretation.

I am very privileged and grateful to Professor Dr Ravin Thatte, M.S. FRCS (Edinburgh) for so kindly agreeing to my request to write a Foreword for this book. I could not have found a more appropriate person than him for not only being a medical specialist of repute but a deep thinker and interpreter in his own right as an authority on the philosophy of 'Srimad Bhagwad Geeta' and 'Dnyaneshwari' by Sant Dnyaneshwar, through extensive writings, books and series of lectures delivered on various platforms within and outside India.

I am particularly indebted to my wife Mrs. Sulochana Moharir, my daughter Mrs. Prachi Moharir Bajaj and brothers Mr. Vijay Moharir and Late Dr. Vasant Moharir for all their inputs, necessary encouragement and for infusing courage and confidence to indulge myself, into such difficult, socio-psychologically complex, at times controversial and most-often emotionally challenging concepts, prevalent in human psyche for thousands of years and to share them with those interested in the form of this book. It is only its readers, who would decide how far I have succeeded in my efforts. I have my pleasure in presenting it in their hands.

Anil Vishnu Moharir

New Delhi
Dated : 13 December 2016

Key Words: *Soul, Ancient Concept, History, Energy-Matter Relationships, Modern Scientific Views, Electric Universe, Consciousness as attribute of Electric Charge, A Multidisciplinary Review.*

PREFACE TO THE SECOND EDITION

Ever since the publication of the first edition of the book in 2017, the author has received several comments, appreciation, messages, accolades, suggestions and congratulations from some of the most learned individuals, known for their enlightened scholarship and knowledge on the book for its being an unusually rare, multidisciplinary, thoughtfully researched and in-depth review on one of the most complex, contested, conflicting, enigmatic and unresolved subjects of Soul and Rebirth for over five thousand years or more. All these scholarly, critical comments have strengthened my confidence, conviction and faith on the line of my thinking, approach, views and critically logical, multidisciplinary interpretation of these ancient concepts in the light of the modern developments in physical sciences, technology, cosmology, stellar chemistry, space science, information, communication, neurology, genetics and molecular and evolutionary biology. I am afraid, never before *(at least to my knowledge)* such a comprehensive <u>multi-disciplinary</u>, scientific review on the subjects of Soul, Rebirth, Work and the Theory of Karma had ever been presented and published earlier. Still however, during the last two years, the author has come to gather some more pertinent, scholarly, research articles and books, which not only support the original premises presented in the first edition of the book, but have induced a compulsive urge in the mind to present all that information for my enlightened readers at the earliest. This is therefore the provision for bringing out a revised, enlarged and updated version at such a short interval. I hope, these efforts would not only bridge the apparent gaps, bring more clarity in understanding the connectivity between several scientific disciplines that are involved in the appreciation, comprehension and interpretation of such complex concepts as soul, rebirth, work and the law of karma. Whereas, most of the text material is essentially the same, some of the paragraphs have been either simplified, enlarged with more information, evidence, explanation or with elaborated interpretation. A new chapter on 'Work, its Origin, Kinds and the Law of Karma: An Attempted Synthesis for their Scientific Foundation and Human Obligations' has been incorporated to emphasize that doing perpetual work is ingrained as an integral part for universal survival of material (animate and inanimate) from their origin / birth to death. In this process, a continued relevance of the Oriental concept of 'The Law of Karma' and the dependence of all material forms (animate and inanimate) on it, have been re-emphasized in the light of modern science. Some views on the mechanisms of the 'inherited karma *(Prarabdh Karma)*' and the 'accumulated karma *(Sanchit Karma)*' and their causative consequential implications in life have been attempted to be explained on the basis of the structure, self-replication, function and modification of the De-oxyribonucleic acid (DNA) program by absorbing new experiences (work) gained by the cells / organisms in responding to the changing epigenetic environment, from the moment of their birth to death. The whole effort is directed to bring about a clear <u>scientific understanding</u>, increased comprehension and related interconnections on the subjects of soul, rebirth and karma in an integrated way. It is also attempted to emphasize, that 'Soul' and 'Rebirth' are certainly not the metaphysical entities as have been given to believe (or interpreted) for thousands of years but in fact the physical realties when explained logically on modern scientific basis. It is believed that readers will appreciate the efforts made on the part of the author to sincerely build up a comprehensive, multidisciplinary, scientific understanding of the ancient concepts of Soul, Rebirth and the Law of Karma and support his appeal to bring about a global consensus on these concepts, purely on the basis of scientific merits, without any kind of bias, prejudice or dogmatic influence from religion, theology, faith or blind faith at the back of the reader's mind. It is sincerely believed that in the twenty first century, wherein science, information and technology are influencing the mind, thought, behaviour and life of the common man, it is imperative on the part of scientists (from all disciplines), philosophers, religious leaders, religious scholars and preachers (of all faiths) to pause and ponder, critically review the tenets of their centuries old religious texts, rationalize their continued relevance and re-interpret them in the light of modern developments in science, technology and biology. Meta-Narrative religious books must essentially be open to moderation with developments in science and technology, incorporation of something new and fundamental and in no case remain perpetually blind and closed to new knowledge and realities. There is no relevance or necessity of teaching the redundant concept, that the Earth is the center of the universe, just because it was, at one point of time, an important statement in the Holy Book –The Bible. In this context, it is comforting to note that the Vatican Pope has accepted the modern theories on 'Evolution' and 'Creation of the universe-The Big Bang' as scientific truths and permit his religious preachers (Male and Female) to even get married. This is indeed a clarion call to all Heads, leaders and preachers of various other religious faiths, irrespective of nationality, for immediate action to pull the humanity out of continued ignorance and wilderness. Humanity has long been kept ridden and languishing in blind faith, orthodoxy, religious obstinacy, dogmatic belief system, pseudo supremacy of one religion over other, fear and phobia of a social need for religious cohesiveness, compulsive control for collective solidarity and collective security. It is time to build a new order of 'Global Religion' essentially based on science, technology, scientific attitude, temper and mindset. The discoverer of the structure of the DNA, Sir Francis Crick (NL) had observed- "Now is the time to think scientifically about consciousness (and its relationship, if any to the hypothetical immortal soul) and most important of all, the time to start the experimental study of consciousness in a serious deliberate way." And the present book fulfills the desire expressed by Sir Francis Crick (NL) in perhaps the best possible way to date.

All the tree chapters of the book have been kept independent with reference material for the convenience of the readers. They can be read independent of each other. Some amount of repetition is therefore unavoidable and readers would excuse this. Moreover, in view of the extreme complexities and inter-relationships involved between these ancient concepts, particularly in view of varied terminologies used by many people in essentially describing the same entity. The underlying connecting linkage between these concepts often becomes blurred. The author strongly feels that a rudimentary understanding or familiarity of basic ancient concepts of Vedic philosophy and popular modern scientific terminology on the part of the reader will facilitate his understanding the subject content of the present book.

The author acknowledges with gratitude the help given by Prof. Dr. Ravin L. Thatte, M.S. FRCS (Edin.), Mumbai, Dr. T. P. Rajendran, Ph.D., New Delhi and Dr. Vidyadhar Gopal Oke, M.B.B.S., M.D., Thane, for reviewing the draft manuscript of the chapter on work and suggesting suitable changes and other inputs. The author is grateful to Swami Suparnanand Maharaj, Secretary and Chairman, Ramkrishna Math Institute of Culture, Kolkata for spontaneously agreeing and obliging me by writing a foreword for this revised second edition of my book.

I am also indebted and grateful to my wife Mrs. Sulochana Anil Moharir (nee- Sulochana Balkrishna Thakar) for not only her support and encouragement but for sparing me from botherations of domestic responsibilities and allowing plenty of time in compiling this book in time.

New Delhi
Dated: 12 July 2019
Ashadh Ekadashi

Anil Vishnu Moharir

Key Words: *Ancient Concept of Soul, Rebirth, History, Energy-Matter Relationships, Modern Scientific Views, Electric Universe, Consciousness as attribute of Electric Charge, Work, Law of Karma, Human Obligations, Multidisciplinary Review*

LORD DATTATREYA

Lord Dattatreya (Figure 1) symbolizes the combined manifestation of the three forces of nature that generate, sustain and destroy all material creation in the Universe. Modern physics recognizes four forces in nature namely; weak interaction, strong interaction, gravitation and electromagnetism. With weak and strong interactions being essentially of similar kind and nature except in the range of their operation between sub-atomic particles present within nuclei of atoms, Lord Dattatreya (Composite of Bramha (Electron), Vishnu (Proton) and Mahesh (Neutron) corresponding to the Creator, Protector and Destroyer Or as is generally understood as the personified

Generator, Operator and Destroyer- GOD) represents the factual reality of only three forces which are primarily responsible for creation, sustenance and destruction of all inanimate and animate material in nature. The operative parts of these three primary forces for action in the Indian philosophy have been depicted and symbolized by their three corresponding female deities, namely, Saraswati with Bramha, Lakshmi with Vishnu and Parvati with Mahesh or Shiva. Saraswati, the operative counterpart of Bramha the creator therefore symbolizes the presiding deity for rhythm, rhythmic periodicity, harmony, peace, tranquility, learning, wisdom and knowledge. This is clearly obvious because it is our common experience that no orderly creative work (construction, structure formation etc) can ever be accomplished without these requirements being in place. In short, without, harmony, peace, rhythm, knowledge and wisdom, Bramha cannot create anything. And Bramha is primarily responsible for bringing about every specific material creation from the atoms of only 118 different kinds available in the universe. And all atoms as the fundamental quantum entity, constitute perpetual harmonic oscillators. Vishnu, the sustainer of creation represents the highest universal cosmic electric potential energy. Vishnu means one who pervades. One who enters into everything that is existing in material form. So he is the transcendent as well as the immanent reality of the universe. He is the inner cause and power by which everything in the universe exists. Higher the electrostatic potential energy, higher is the capacity to create and perform work (creation) and consequently higher the scope for generating material wealth. Modern physics tells us that no material structure (animate or the inanimate) is possible to exist without electric charge, which pervades the entire cosmos. And Vishnu signifies the all pervading universal electrostatic charge continuum. The electron (negatively charged particle) is primarily responsible for the combination of different atoms together to form molecules of various kinds of material structures and therefore signifies the Bramha. No surprise, why Bramha is always depicted to be seated on the lotus flower (a symbol of energy) stemming out from the navel of Vishnu in the Hindu literature. The whole universe today is known to be electrical in nature. That leads me to think that it may indeed be the 'electric charge' that most possibly represents the enigmatic entity called 'Soul' which, we have been searching for and holding dear to our hearts for thousands of years? It is our common knowledge that even highest electrostatic potential generated need orderly regulation and control for its flow through step- up or step-down transformers and grid systems for distribution to various locations to make it produce useful work. Therefore, Mahalakshmi or Lakshmi, the counterpart female deity of Vishnu (universal cosmic electrostatic potential energy) obviously symbolizes wealth because it is only with higher accumulation of potential energy and its controlled regulation, there is any possibility to generate the capacity to perform work and create wealth and prosperity. Lastly, Mahesh or Shiva being the mighty destroyer symbolizes the Gravitational force in nature which is often destructive. It is the root cause of the accumulation of matter in the universe and for all disturbances as a result of such accumulation on cosmic scale in the universe. The dormant potential state of this mighty force of nature within human body has been symbolized by the 'Kundalini' that lies at the base of the spinal cord. Everything concerned with human spirituality and spiritual life call it by whatever name such as; samadhi, maha-samadhi, nirvana, moksha, communion, union, kaivalya, liberation, bliss or tranquility, is related to the awakening of 'Kundalini' within body. Active Manifestation of 'Kundalini' force, depending upon the purpose of its use; in potential capacity generation, continued sustenance or abrupt destruction, are known respectively by the names of – Mahalakshmi, Saraswati and Parvati. No wonder the female operative counterpart of gravitational force should be represented by the most fearful, ruthless, lightening-like quick, abrupt and thunderously chaotic deity in action, called by the name of Parvati. Other variations of this force are known by the names of Rudrani (Kali), Maha-Kali, Chandi, Mahishasura Mardini or Durga. In the Tantrik literature, when Kundalini force is awakened but cannot be handled, it is called the Kali. When it can be handled and used for some beneficial purpose and we become powerful on account of it, it is called the Durga. Both, Kali or Durga, because of their unpredictable potential destructive power are the most worshiped, feared and appeased deities for seeking protection to life and property. Both Kali and Durga are indeed the attributes of inner states of human mind / physiology / psychology and behavior. (For more detailed description, the readers are directed to read- 'Kundalini Tantra' by Swami Satyanand Saraswati, Yoga Publication Trust, Munger, Bihar, India). The trinity- of Bramha, Vishnu and Mahesh (Shiv) along with their female counterparts always remain in operation in nature together in tandem and coherence. In case of any weakening of any one of these three forces under any circumstances, the relatively stronger of the remaining two forces becomes the dominant one and its effect is visualized in action as per its basic nature. In an attempt to seek the scientific truth and meaning contained in the symbolic representation, observation of above correlations between the concept of the Lord Dattatreya from the Indian Philosophy with modern theory of the physical structure of matter, we only feel dismayed with owe and nothing else.

A Hindu Tantric Painting. India, Pahari, circa 1780-1800.
Depicting from top to bottom: Shiva, Sakti, Vishnu on
his conch with Brahma sprouting from his navel and Lakshmi,
Harihara, four-headed Brahma, and the Trimurti below,
painted against a gold ground forming the stylized
seed syllable Ohm, surrounded by a dark blue floral border
with gold painted scrollwork.

'Bramha-Saraswati', 'Vishnu-Lakshmi' and 'Shiva-Parvati' and Dattatreya, depicted together in the above painting (Figure 2) against the background of the primordial harmonically resonating cosmic sound, symbolized by 'OM' and constituting the three fundamental forces in nature, which are responsible for all material creation, their sustenance and finally destruction in the universe. *(Reproduced with apology from an unspecified source available on the internet)*

(The above write-up is meant for favour of consideration, introspection and serious discussion by the readers with or without any formal scientific training with the sole objective of arousing scientific curiosity and promoting awareness and attitude to at least invoke people to look to our ancient concepts from purely scientific point of view. In doing so, I may perhaps be incorrect for the time being but who knows, someone from somewhere, taking this as a clue, may discover and establish the factual scientific truth and understanding behind such ancient concepts?)

Anil Vishnu Moharir

Figure 3. Statuette of 'Ardha-Nari-Nateshwar'

As a composite of equal halves of masculine Shiva (left) and feminine Parvati (right).

Most possibly a symbolic representation of the existence of 'Supersymmetry' in nature predicted by the modern 'Standard Model of Particle Physics'. For that matter, masculine Bramha and feminine Saraswati and masculine Vishnu and feminine Lakshmi represent the other two 'supersymmetric' forces of nature.

For discussion see text under description on supersymmetry (p. 23-24)

CHAPTER 1
A Scientific Look at the Concept of Soul: An Attempted Synthesis

1.1 ABSTRACT

This small book traces the developments in efforts to recognize and difficulties encountered in understanding the enigmatic phenomenon of Soul, life after death and reincarnation being discussed for over 5,000 years of human history and yet being far away from a global consensus. The reasons are more of religious dogma, religious pride, religious divide, blind faith, false sense of superiority of one religion over others, and perhaps above all; fear and lack of courage on the part of people to cross the carefully erected religious and social barriers arising out of 'meta-narrative' books and their interpretations to rebel in favour of scientific logic, reason, arguments and truth. Despite tremendous developments in material sciences, elementary particle physics, space science and technology and modern molecular biology, our understanding of the enigmatic concept of Soul, its meaning, nature, constitution, structure, function and physical location within body in relation to environment, physiology, psychology, biochemistry, thought process, concept and nature of memory and physical behavior are still not known in a holistic way. The author argues against the old concept of 'Soul' taking its permanent residence within the body of an organism from the moment of birth until it exits on death. It has been logically argued that instead of taking a permanent residence inside a body, the so called conscious individual 'Soul' actually remains in continual connection on its own with the universal consciousness (electric potential continuum) from the moment of conception, development, birth to its final death by means of 'electric charge' mediated through millions of ion channels in the bodies of living organisms. Whenever the physical body of any living organism from the unicellular bacteria to the most evolved of all species the human being is incapacitated for the sustained flow of electric charge / universal consciousness / ionic movements within itself to drive electric currents through specific ion-channels in motivating the conscious body, death occurs. Death, at least in any multi-cellular organism is therefore not an instantaneous process but a gradual withdrawal of consciousness as a result of progressive closing of ion-channels from various organs / parts in a sequential order. The Vedic concept and structural model for the Soul, described about 8,000 years BC, has been briefly described and logically discussed in relation to the developments in modern physical and biological science and known facts about life to assert that everything attributed to and described about the qualities and properties of the so called 'Soul' are also factually true about the- 'Electric Charge'. Therefore, there is merit in assuming that under dogmatic influences of religious beliefs descended down to us through hundreds of centuries, and repeated by millions of influential religious preachers and stalwarts through millennia of historical past, we have perhaps lost courage to neither question / review / logically argue nor introspect, and failed to recognize 'Electric Charge' to be the de-facto 'Soul' that not only drives the entire universe but also the living world on earth, irrespective of its terrestrial, aquatic or plant origins. Still however, until a global consensus is built up on scientific merits, the Vedic concept of Soul stands tall and provides a logical, quasi-scientific explanation to satisfy human curiosity to a great extent. The task of compiling a comprehensive review article with a purely scientific outlook about such a complex subject as Soul from a multidisciplinary point of view was a daunting task. In doing so, it is very difficult to expect that all readers of this book will have a uniformly common multi-disciplinary and socio-religious background, comprehension and understanding besides willingness to welcome and consider radically new thoughts on the ancient concepts. Still, it is believed that the readers in general and scientific community in particular, would appreciate the efforts with an open, unbiased mind and read something unconventional because it is not so easy for any individual to break away from our dogmatic emotional views, ideas and prejudices, acquired and held dear to heart from grooming since childhood.

A Scientific Look at the Concept of Soul: An Attempted Synthesis

1.2 Introduction and Background Information

Scientific explorations at mental and spiritual levels had begun ever since human beings learnt to observe, think and analytically interact with his surroundings. And this period, on the basis of authentic recorded history, dates back to at least 25,000 years BC in India and the Vedic civilization that followed [1-3]. This also initiated in human beings, a quest for an understanding of their own position and purpose, within the scheme of natural material creation. Man began to explore; who he actually is? What is his constitution and composition? Where from and how he has come into being? What is his relation to the other living species on the Earth? What is the purpose of his existence? What is his final destination? Where is that destination located? And out of several apparently deceptive self-images, what is his real identity? What is materially common between him and surrounding life forms and other life-less objects? From his birth to his death-bed, he observed several irreversibly changing phases in his own life? But the so called 'I' or 'Me' within the frame of his body, from birth to death has been believed to have remained the same despite drastic changes in external appearance with time and age. Who is this 'I' or 'Me' inside the body? Why is there the death and why is there birth? What is the meaning of 'death' and that of 'birth'? Modern developments in physical science tell us that everything in the universe is made up of atoms, the smallest particles of matter which exist in 118 different specific kinds. The atoms are built up from sub-atomic particles the protons, neutrons and electrons, which in turn are made up of the fundamental elementary particles called the 'quarks' or possibly from the elementary particles originating from energy of the magnetic monopoles. Two or more, similar or dissimilar atoms combine together with the help of their negatively charged electrons to form structures of various kinds, nature, characteristics and properties and they include both the animate and the inanimate world. After specific period of time, or under specific epigenetic environmental conditions, all these animate and the inanimate structures naturally disintegrate into their individual component atoms or groups of atoms to return to nature and are recycled to form new entities. This cycle of formation of structures and their disintegration is continuing in a perpetual way because of the infinite types of energy that abound in 'space' ever since and from even before the material universe came into being. And this 'space' can be atomic, molecular, planetary, galactic or universal. The energy undoubtedly is limitless and un-ending. Recycling of material formed by the chemical combination of various kinds of atoms is a universal law of nature and can only be explained with practical examples. The real miraculous recycling is exemplified by the subtle occurrences that take place within each living organism on this earth. And the most efficient chemical recycling in nature takes place between the plants and animals and in the miracle of the rebirth of essential gases to start the cycle of life via the solar photonic rays [4]. We now know for sure that it is the number of electrically neutral neutrons, positive protons and negatively charged electrons that provide consciousness, individual identity, integrity and existence to each of the 118 kinds of atoms as to who they are? And these atoms retain their individual indentity, despite being perpetually recycled in nature. Obviously therefore, the concept of a definite life-span, fate and destiny must have emerged from the varying intervals of time observed for different materials (both animate and inanimate) between the moment of their creation to their disintegration. Everything in the universe from movement of stellar constellations to galaxies, planets, and planetary motions, rotation of earth and its moon around the Sun, to occurrence of the day and night cycles as well as the seasons on earth are therefore observed to be cyclic and periodic. No surprise, like every other phenomenon in nature, it was but natural to also ask if events like 'death' and 'birth' in animate objects in nature are also cyclic? So far as the question of all animate organisms, as a part of the natural material creation is concerned, recycling of their constituent material after death is well understood. But, if every individual man / woman (and in this context, possibly every kind of life form) is also destined to return back to birth in a cyclic phase after his / her death, as is popularly believed, then obviously a series of other questions come to mind. How? When? Where? Which form and sex of a living being? And after what interval of time is this return possible? What conditions determine our return in a re-birth? And most obviously whether those conditions are self-organized, and if not, then by whom or under what physical or environmental conditions and circumstances does that happen? What happens to the 'I' or the 'Me' in the body? Whether this identity 'I' or 'Me' is carried forward to the next birth? Whereas, in a majority of cases children forget and do not remember the identity of their past life after birth, thousands of case studies have been recorded from all over the world wherein, children, predominantly in the age group of 2-6 years, distinctly remember their past births [4-8]. Where, does this 'I' or 'Me' stay after death and in what form and conditions? What is conscious memory about the 'I' or the 'Me' and what is its vehicle? How and where this memory is located, gets recorded and recalled? What or who keeps record of this memory? Is it recorded by the 'I' or 'Me' **(as metaphysical entity)** that is believed to live within or by any of the several organ parts of the body? When bodies of the past lives are physically burned or destroyed, how then does the memory get transported and recalled after rebirth as has been observed and reported from all parts of the world? Obviously therefore, memory cannot be something materially physical. And for that matter, the possibility of genes (DNA) carrying the memory **(of conscious individual identity)** is scientifically impossible because genetic memory essentially requires an unbroken physical transfer of genetic material from one life to the other of the same individual. Scientific observation and logic about past-birth memory indicates that genetic explanation for transfer of memory from one life to the next is not possible. Obviously, it can be assumed that it may be the non-destructible, metaphysical entities- 'I' or the 'Me' within bodies that must be carrying memories of past births with it. And if this is so; then it is curious to know the structure, form and make-up of this so called 'I' or the 'Me' and where and how within it, the memories of life are stored, recorded and transported to the next births? These questions have been repeatedly raised by philosophers, thinkers, religious leaders and research scientists through thousands of years of human history without coming to a definite, unanimous and universally accepted answer. **Actually, few thousand isolated cases of individuals, claimed to be remembering their past-births, are statistically very insignificant or negligible in comparison to several billions of others who just do not remember anything of their past lives.** Howsoever insignificant, it is a tribute to the integrity of the scientist community that they do not want to leave anything for chance and every single anamorphous incidence is subjected to a rigorous scientific scrutiny. And yet, there is no conclusive scientific proof of rebirths of any individual from the historical past is evident. Moreover, nearly 50% human population on earth today have no religious tradition to believe in rebirth and a substantial majority from them are quite agnostic about its possibility. Still however, if we claim or intuitively feel that some form of identity as 'soul' persists beyond death, it becomes necessary to know what stuff or particles is that 'soul' made of ? Is it materialistic or non-materialistic by nature? Is it real or merely an illusion? What forces hold it together within a body and allow it to exhibit its conscious attributes? And how does it interact with ordinary matter? These are some of the questions that need to be explained on the basis of scientific reason and logic. **Alternately, a logical explanation for the origin, assembly, manifestation, reproduction and exhibition of all attributes of a conscious living beings has to be found and explained from the characteristics, properties and behavior of their constituent atomic or molecular material and we should be open to consider, discuss and accept such new interpretations.**

William Grassie *(In Chapter 7, 'The New Science of Religion: Exploring Spirituality from the Outside In and Bottom Up', Palgrave Macmillan, 2010)* argues that there is a deep narrative structure of human thought and it is through this narrative that we create and recreate our selfhood and that 'self' is a product of our telling and not some essence to be delved in the recesses of subjectivity. Narratives not only create for individuals their inner and social selves; narratives are also what bind societies and cultures together by inducing similar thoughts and thereby creating similar ideologies. They help us to integrate events and actions over a period of time into meaningful patterns, specify cause-and-effect relationships and organize them into coherent wholes. It is the narratives which tell us which events and actions are significant and which can be ignored. The narratives again explain the inter-relationships of all events in our lives. And our moral reasoning is not a matter of our propositional logic and rational choice but a product based on the analogical application of powerful narrative stories (fed to our imagination in our grooming from childhood) to new situations in the course of our life. In short, it is only the exercise in a certain nesting of stories and stories- within- stories together all the way down. The most of important stories, which humans tell, re-tell, re-frame and circulate for generations, are not even consciously recognized at all to be only stories. These master stories called the 'meta-narratives' are the stuff of ideologies, religions, nationalisms, faiths, sects and cultures that form the unarticulated background, emotional modulations and conditioning of our "taken-forgranted truth". And once captured and entrenched in the minds of people, these 'meta-narratives' become difficult to rationalize or refute. They structure our thoughts, personality, beliefs and behavior in many profound ways. It is this background which is responsible for our prejudices, biases and social choices. In general, people surrender their ability to doubt and think independently for themselves. No wonder, why discussions on religion or politics between people with widely different beliefs very often generate heat, rage and even violence. By virtue of habit, people tend to choose facts based on 'meta-narratives' and carefully interpret them to new situations. No surprise therefore that whenever 'meta-narrative' books have been forbidden for updating, revision, editing, correction or a new interpretation in the light of advancements in science and technology, there follows a certain confusion, frustration, regimentation, irrationality, dogmatism and obstinate adherence to ritualistic traditions and intolerance to new thoughts amongst their believers and followers. The situation often turns explosive in dealing with the followers of any organized religion or faith.

1.3 Necessity of a scientific theory for life after-death / reincarnation

In this connection from times immemorial, several theories have been proposed and explanations given by many persons from all over the world but surprisingly, not a single theory enjoys universal acceptance. Natural laws of creation of the living world and process for birth and death in humans are universally common, irrespective of physical location on the Earth, environmental and climatic conditions at the place of birth, colour of skin, race, blood-group type, level of education or literacy and such other considerations. In this respect, therefore, there are no separate laws for different nationalities, communities or races. **The Science of human birth and death does not recognize differences between religious faiths because, the structural make-up and the kind of various organs, physical appearance and forms, physiological, biochemical, metabolic, mental, emotional and psychological thought processes are identical, irrespective of location, colour of skins and external features.** Not a single case of sexual infertility has ever been reported from marriages between partners observing different religious faiths. If there are natural scientific laws which can be logically and adequately used, within statistical limits of accuracy and probability, to understand and explain the entire process of creation, properties, functions, differences, corrective measures and sustainability of the living and non-living material world, then there is no reason why a universally acceptable theory or explanation cannot be sought or arrived at, on the questions regarding life, its origin, death, birth and re-birth because the entire community of conscious living organisms (inclusive of all unicellular, multi-cellular and multi-organ organisms) shares a common gene-pool, planet for heritage, dwelling and destiny. Such a theory should however be based purely on merits of scientific truth, logic, reason and free from dogmatic personal or social bias towards religious opinions, blind-faiths, allegiance, influences, prejudices or any other commercial or social vested interests. **Even Albert Einstein admitted that- "We believe that science serves humanity best when it is all free of influence by any dogma and reserves the right to question all assumptions, including their own" and "It is more difficult to break a prejudice than an atom".**

Human beings observe and follow particular faith or religion mainly because of parental nurture and grooming in childhood and also a certain family or social structure rather than as an independently chosen personal option. Once adapted to a particular thought, or a ritual, it stays as a habit with the person all his / her life. More particularly, faiths in general are being mechanically followed as unconscious victims of mob-psychology or more particularly due to morphic resonance of social morphic fields, as described by Rupert Sheldrake [9-12] and arising out of strong community feelings and identity, sense of insecurity, a constant fear of something unknown, lack of self-confidence, lack of freedom and courage to cross social structural and ideological boundaries and incapacity for independent thinking to reason outside the frame of grooming since birth. These fields interact with each other among different individual members of the same species and are reasons for a collective coordinated behavior of individual members e.g. coordinated formation of birds during flights, swimming of fishes in schools, behavior of individual human beings in a crowd etc. **Sheldrake theorizes that living morphic-fields simultaneously exist in the past, present and future and govern both human and animal behavior, forming a living matrix upon which the physical bodies are formed** [11]. Therefore, such conscious or unconscious victimization and submission to mechanical ritualistic following of any religion / faith is visible in all communities across the world and has been very well documented by Richard Dawkins [12] and by Robert Hinde [13] as a result of his Gallup poll in the United States in which three quarters of staunch Catholics and Protestants could not name a single Old Testament prophet, more than two-thirds did not know who preached the sermon on the mount and an equal number thought that Mosses was one of the twelve apostles of Jesus. A similar situation exists amongst the followers of all other faiths or religions.

Many faiths such as Christianity and Islam *(with a common origin)* deny the possibility of human life after-death / rebirth more as a religious dogma than for any sound scientific logic, despite the holy book being known to be an axiom and not the end product of a process of scientific reasoning. And yet, the book was always vehemently upheld to be true. Moreover, in some cases where the evidence seemed to contradict it, it is the evidence that was preferred to be thoughtlessly thrown out without question, reason or introspection and not the book. It is a historical fact that reincarnation was an accepted part of Judaism into which Jesus himself was born. The original texts of both the Old and the New Testaments indeed contained references to life after-death and reincarnation but they were consciously and deliberately removed in **A.D. 325** by the Roman emperor Constantine the Great and his mother Helena. The Second Ecumenical Council of Constantinople meeting in **A.D. 553** confirmed and endorsed their action declaring the concept of reincarnation as a heresy but more objectively as a possible ulterior threat to the growing power and hegemony of the Church [14] if people were allowed to logically think and keep independent opinions. Scientific truth of the planet Earth not being the center of the universe was opposed for hundreds of years by the dogmatic Christian Church, purely on blind faith. Eminent independent thinkers, who opposed the view of the Church were forced to abandon their views and opinion, persecuted, tortured or forced to drink poison and accept death. No wonder, universal, unanimous acceptability for any scientifically logical theory on Soul, re-birth or life after-death has always been made difficult, not because there is no such theory in existence which logically attempts to explain all the phenomenon mentioned above but only because, our social, political and religious leaders since time immemorial from all nationalities, consciously or unconsciously, purposefully or otherwise have been only dividing humanity into factions of races, groups of religious faiths, in the name of supremacy of one faith over others and thereby setting individuals, against accepting such a theory in the name of faith or allegiance or loyalty to a religion, that does not subscribe to such ideas and more particularly for fear of inviting wrath of the mighty powerful ruler or the unknown GOD as a creator. **Therefore, for the time being, there are no relevant reasons for either accepting or summarily rejecting the concept of 'Soul' or 'reincarnation' until they are thoroughly contested on the basis of modern scientific logic and reason. And they continue to be a question of blind dogmatic faith or belief and disbelief, a mental block, vested interest or lack of conviction and courage to impartially uphold a possible logical scientific truth.**

As an example, Christianity did not subscribe to Earth being an ordinary planet that revolves around the Sun but had to abandon its dogma because they could no longer hold people bound to their views against scientific truth and logic. The sole purpose in doing all this being to sow seeds of confusion, kill the capacity and initiatives of individuals for independent thinking and judicious evaluation based on scientific reason and logic besides imposing curbs on intellectual freedom by way of polarizing the minds of the lay population. No wonder, there have been innumerable cases of coercion, regimentation, detentions, engineered riots, physical killing and eliminations of those who rebelled against such orthodox systems put in place by vested socio-economic-religious power groups. The very fact that because both Christianity and Islam right from the time they attempted to propagate professional religion, did not advocate belief in re-birth as a basic tenet of their philosophy, not much thinking was either allowed to be done in this direction, or it was physically curbed or actively destroyed by the followers of both these faiths. It is also a well known historical fact that both Christianity and Islam have been propagated more on the might of the sword and dogmatism. This is exemplified by Edgar Cayce [15], a psychic clairvoyant, who would place himself into a self-hypnotic trance to give healing relief to mentally and psychologically disturbed people and was convinced that the reasons for certain specific condition of a person was due mainly to memories of his / her past life influences. Despite this self-realization, Edgar Cayce who was a devout Christian by faith, did not dare to honestly profess or conscientiously share his self-realized truth in public but merely confined himself to silently practicing 'Life Readings' of affected people. Today, more and more people from the Western world and about 30% people in the United States despite their faith in Christianity, are believing in 'life-after-death' and reincarnation. Sufis, the esoteric branch of Islam and Hasidic Judaism support reincarnation and so also the Gnostic and mystical traditions of Christianity. Outside the religion, Pythagoras, Plato, David Hume, Ralph Waldo Emerson, Henry Thoreau, Benjamin Franklin, J.W. von Goethe and Sir Isaac Newton all were known to have believed in reincarnation.

Hypnotic regression (which is supposedly or erroneously believed to push patients to go into their past births?) is being increasingly used these days by psychologists and psychotherapists as a regular therapy to cure patients ridden with chronic mental depression, hallucinations, fear and traumatic phobia of knives, rivers, oceans and water bodies, mountain heights, vehicles, trains, aero-planes and such other problems with successful return of their patients to live their normal lives after erasing the causative metabolic, physiological or genetic reasons or memory of their fear and phobia but believed to be inherited from past lives [5]. Not only this, when hypnotically regressed into their past memories (lives?), people at times have been reported to speak in languages completely unknown to them in the present lives. In this context, Marcus Tillius Cicero (106-43 BC), the Roman philosopher maintained that the fact our children grasp certain abilities and skills at surprising speeds is a strong proof of their knowing those skills before birth and that genius is nothing but only flowering of experience from the previous life. Such abilities in picking knowledge and learning find easy explanation in the theory of life-after-death. So also the reasons and explanation for differences in aptitude and abilities between children (including twins) born to same parents with identical genetic heritage may have an explanation in the hypothesis of life-after-death [16]. If this is true, then it remains to understand how incidental memories, experiences and skills acquired in previous lives are transferred to the present life without physical transfer of the genetic molecule-DNA through successive procreations. Perhaps, we need to re-look at the DNA, at its anti-parallel asymmetric structure, total number in each organism, types, process of replication, operation, function or some hidden dimensions (if any?) of these self-replicating molecules of life from an entirely different perspective [17]. There appears to be some other (hitherto unknown) mode for transfer of memories, information, experiences and skills from one generation to the other. And this process may altogether be independent of the structural makeup of the DNA and even more likely, without physical necessity of rebirth of an individual as a precondition. Intensive polarization of thoughts within groups of persons, through repeated dialogues, discussions and discourses with influential preachers or by reading emotionally captivating meta-narrative books are some of the most important modes for transfer of memories to multiple individuals. Therefore, alternately, the role of the 'Morphic Fields and their resonance' that simultaneously transcend through the past, present and future in the transfer of memory, experience and skill, as proposed by Rupert Sheldrake [9-12] deserve a far more serious consideration. Fields, resonances and their causative effects on matter and its behavior can be easily correlated with the fundamental nature, properties and characteristic vibrations of the atoms and molecules from which the entire Universe (both animate and inanimate) has come into being. Questions about our continued belief in the theory of rebirth have recently been critically discussed by the author of this book elsewhere [18] and the same has also been included as an independent chapter (Ch.2) in the present book. On the other hand, Professor Dick Frans Swaab, a researcher of international repute on human brain indicates * (Ref – "We are our Brains: From the womb to Alzheimer's" Penguine Books, 2014, Translated by Jane Headley-Prole) that all phenomena such as; NDE (near death experiences), re-experiencing panoramic memories of events that had taken place several decades earlier in the past, epilepsy, experiencing spiritual or religious feelings of being in unison with universe, world, or God, or thought of having gone to heaven or experiencing the feeling of being in direct contact with God, Jesus, or some other religious figure, the feeling of peace and tranquility, absence of pain, the vision of going through a long tunnel and all such experiences are in fact the results of some kind of impairment of brain function, inducing a state between consciousness and deep sleep and unconsciousness. Several other reasons such as; severe blood loss, septic or anaphylactic shock (severe allergic reactions), electrocution, going into coma due to brain damage or cerebro-vascular accident, suicide, near drowning and depression, excessive levels of carbon dioxide, hyperventilation, LSD, psilocybin or mescaline (hallucinogens) and sudden or too rapid acceleration to higher altitudes in fighter jet planes have also been reported to induce such experiences. An out of body experience can be triggered by stimulating the place where the temporal lobe and the parietal lobe meet in the brain. Use of cannibalis, which influences a great many chemical messengers in the brain, electrical stimulation near the fornix at the rear of the hypothalamus gland also activates the experience of recalling events that had taken place several decades earlier. This area has been earmarked to be storing episodic autobiographical memories that form the chronicle of our lives. Moreover, being extremely sensitive to lack of oxygen, it can be easily be activated. Likewise, stimulation of hippocampus provokes extremely clear, highly detailed autobiographical memories including memories of people who have died [19].

1.4 Dawn of the scientific and industrial revolution and implication

The dawn of modern scientific and industrial revolution in the closing years of the nineteenth century, initiated an assertive process of definition, evaluation, calibration of all units of physical quantities and their measurement, followed by universal standardization of material characterization, applications and mass industrial production with a consequent improvement in the quality of human life. These developments have lead to accepting and adopting science and technology as the vehicles of change for economic prosperity, reducing inequalities and global socialization. The scientific thought process founded on the philosophical basis of Rene Descartes, Lord Francis Bacon's methodology and Sir Isaac Newton's mathematics supported by experimental verification on the basis of logically built hypothesis and theories for explaining any natural phenomena have become the foundations of state policies, besides ensuring quality of governance and livelihood support to citizens at affordable costs. These efforts have not only gone in organizing material natural resources but also in harnessing the seemingly invisible resources in the form of nuclear, space, communication, digital and nano-science technologies. **Today, no one questions or doubts the potential, power, utility and practical application value of physical gadgets that are spinning out from these sciences concerning the invisible but realistic sub-atomic world.** A new era of scientific awareness, willingness to change with open mind for accepting new thoughts, new sciences, new possibilities with consideration and respect for plausible alternate explanations for already known phenomena has dawned. Subjects like consciousness, mind, mind-matter interface and interactions, thoughts and thought waves and their teleportation to distant location, telepathy, distant-vision, clairvoyance, precognition, psycho-kinesis, near-death experiences and after-death reincarnation, bioelectronics, para-physics and para-psychology etc, which were contemptuously held unscientific are no longer forbidden from scientific exploration and enquiry.

Because of developments in science done in the 20th Century, scientists are increasingly getting aware of the universal continuum of information, knowledge, inter-connectivity of sciences and innumerable possibilities of energy-matter interactions and their manifestation as realities. Thanks to the scientific re-confirmation of the fact, known since antiquity that man is a part and parcel of nature and the entire Universe contributes to our life and to what we are, coming through the information gathered with the help of inter-planetary and galactic probes and the Hubble Space Telescope. Scientists are far more willing without any aversion or prejudice to now experimentally explore these areas and even conservative agencies are encouraging research with lavish funding. There is therefore no reason or justification for Religious leaders / Preachers to remain themselves ignorant, aloof, isolated or blind-folded from these developments and also to keep their followers scientifically unaware, ignorant and continue to dogmatically oppose new thinking. They first need to open-up themselves, develop capacity to understand and correlate the new science, evolve with changing time, accept reality and help in providing a scientific basis to the preaching of their faiths (meta-narratives) to newer generations. Because, the only purpose of all religions is to individually and collectively educate and empower their followers to live mentally, emotionally, thoughtfully, intellectually, physiologically, nutritionally, and physically in sound good health and above all socially in harmony with the laws of nature. Depending upon geographical location on Earth, our food intake, its nature and effective digestion, the metabolisms of our bodies are mediated to a great extent by the external environment and religious preachers must help their followers in developing the necessary mental strategies to deal with them for a healthy survival. This is the only meaning, essence, purpose and duty of all religions, past or present that have flourished on the Earth. Perhaps, this may have been the reason why Sir Isaac Newton, emotionally took to preaching religion *(scientific)* at the fag-end of his career in science and mathematics. And he (Newton) is reported to have been appealing for drastic reformation of religion in the practice of the most essential common activity, the human worship of GOD. There is therefore, no scope, logic, reason, wisdom and purpose to pitch one religion or faith against another as rivals. Science and inculcation of scientific attitude and scientific mindset is going to be the only 'New Religion' of the world, irrespective of geographical location or nationalities. No wonder, there appears some truth in the statement of Acharya Rajneesh 'Osho' when he said that- "If religions (old) do not progressively evolve with the time and modern scientific thoughts, they will have no option but to die".

1.5 Everything in the universe is made of atoms: Recycling is the fundamental law of nature

Hydrogen as the basic element in nature constitutes about 80% of our universe. With only one proton and one electron, nuclei of Hydrogen atoms fuse together to produce all other heavier elements found in nature. As the basic element and building blocks from which nuclei of all other 118 different kinds of atomic elements are derived, Hydrogen, expresses the oneness and universal continuum and all other expressions can be reduced to that oneness. However, the exceptional moment that marked the starting point of the development i.e. formation and proliferation of Hydrogen itself in the universe from something that did not materially exist and what conditions triggered this, continues to baffle scientists to date. Hydrogen (proton with unit positive electric charge) corresponds exactly with the cosmic energy of that very moment when the 'Hydrogen proton' as first atomic / sub-atomic material came into being. In other words, Hydrogen is the connecting link in the process of unification with the origin and cosmic center and the enigmatic 'Soul' believed to be manifesting within the living material unit, the biological cell. Hydrogen forms bonds with oxygen atoms and other molecules which are important in many chemical processes, besides being responsible for the unique property of water as an excellent solvent. The water molecule consists of two hydrogen atoms covalently bound to one oxygen atom. Since oxygen is more electronegative than hydrogen, it pulls the shared electron more closely towards itself, making oxygen atom slightly more negative than either of the two hydrogen atoms. This charge imbalance is called a dipole and causes water molecule to have distinct positive and negative polar sides, almost similar to a tiny magnet. Water molecules align themselves so that hydrogen on one molecule will face the oxygen on another molecule. This enables water to acquire greater viscosity and capacity to dissolve other molecules with slightly positive or negative charge. Hydrogen bonds are also primarily responsible for holding the complementary strands of the double helix of the DNA molecules besides determining the three dimensional structures of proteins, enzymes and antibody molecules. It also implies a recognition and awareness of the fact that we are all one with the integration of this cosmic energy at the cellular level. Perhaps the mystery of local and universal consciousness is hidden in the way hydrogen fosters, sustains, maintains and of course mediates the formation of structures through chemical covalent bonds with itself or with any other kinds of elemental atoms, obviously through its negative equivalent of electric charge, the electron [4, 20]. The so called valence electrons of an elemental atom are the real work horse of all the electrons orbiting its nuclei. These valence electrons interact with valence electrons of another atom nearby to foster ionic or covalent bonds between themselves. Ionic bonds are formed as result of transfer of electron from one atom to the other whereas their sharing between the two atoms forms what are called the covalent bonds. Most organic plants and animal substances are formed basically through the carbon atom (C) which creates stable linkages with other atoms such as carbon, oxygen, hydrogen and nitrogen by sharing each other's electrons through covalent bonds. Essentially, this process needs sunlight for their formation. Almost 99% of the atoms in the conscious organic life systems on the Earth are made up of carbon, hydrogen, oxygen and nitrogen. But, as a result of the infinite number of compounds involved, organic life is very complex. Vegetation, which proliferates with carbon dioxide (CO_2) and water (H_2O)

in the presence of photonic energy from the sun, is the starting point of the whole cycle of animate material creation. This solar photonic energy gets translated into the Adenosine Tri-phosphate (ATP) in the photosynthesis process of plants and in hydrolysis of carbohydrates in all animals. Thus, ATP molecules, tracing their origin from the solar energy in fact motivate all plant and animal life forms on the earth. And all these plant and other life forms, from the moment of their birth to the last-breath only lead to a struggle to receive solar energy for their survival. No wonder, the reason as James Morgia [4] describes- "Why everything on this planet earth raises its branches and arms to the Sun." This has been going on since times immemorial and yet, no one knows how it happens. It is only the negatively charged 'Electrons' know how and why it happens and also the true meaning and purpose of recycling of material in nature'. **Therefore, most probably, we may have failed to recognize 'Hydrogen proton' or its negative equivalent the 'Electron' i.e. the electric charge to be the *de-facto* 'Soul' and lost ourselves in the mire of confusion created by our imagination, fanciful invention, fictional descriptions and adventure of assigning arbitrary attributes to several terminologies such as; 'I or the Me' / Self / Soul / Psyche / Astral Body / Conscience / Subtle Body / Spirit / Spiriton / Subconscious / Super-conscious / Voice of the Heart / Atma / Paramatma / Energy-informational matrix / Reactive Mind or a 'Quantum Monod' etc. in essentially describing the same thing popularly known since antiquity as the 'Soul'. It is worth standing away from the madding crowd and orthodox views, pause for while and introspect, if our efforts to realize the enigmatic 'Soul' as we perceive, may not be a proverbial 'chase for the non-existent wild goose'.**

G W Warder [19] in his celebrated book – "The Universe a Vast Electric Organism' also clearly mentions that 'Electric Charge' is the invisible force which evolves from substance and all visible things. **Matter is but the outer garment of these invisible electric forces. It is the Spirit ('the so called 'Soul / electric charge'- my interpretation) which creates psychic life, and makes life the**

cause instead of the consequences of organisms. In fact, flow of electric currents is everywhere, even in human body. Our cells are specialized to conduct electrical currents. Electricity is required for the nervous system to send signals throughout the body and to the brain, making it possible for us to move, think and feel. Sir J. J. Thompson while announcing the discovery of electrons also described them as the common constituent of all matter. Flow of electrons is called the electricity or electric current. It is electricity, which has evolved the physical universe and makes it a vast electric organism, which is bound together by invisible electrical forces and which are the cause instead of the consequence of physical organism [21]. Against a such background of historical developments in this area of subject matter, most of the descriptive (meta-narrative) texts on Soul, contributed by very eminent persons over centuries in the past from various disciplines are indeed a myriad collection of beautifully worded, strongly motivating, emotionally charged, intricately skilled, psychologically captivating, thoughtfully polarizing, mentally paralyzing and yet, profoundly influential literary compositions of scintillating words and phrases, subjectively presenting individual perceptions of these authors / compilers and yet lacking in scientific clarity and details.

Everything in the animate and inanimate material world is made up of 'Atoms' the basic units as 'energy condensates' and building blocks of matter that were created in nuclear furnaces of developing stars about 13.7 billion years ago and are universally available in very limited number of (118) kinds and quantity. Ever since then, the particulate-atoms have maintained their identities and individual characteristic properties [22]. Perhaps the invariable and incorruptible values of the 200+ odd 'physical constants' in nature have maintained the individual identities of these element atoms. Why and how the values of these 'physical constants' are so finely and precisely tuned that makes the existence of the material universe and conscious life-forms on the Earth possible is a perpetual unsolved mystery. We have no means, nor capacity to alter their values and certainly no option but to accept them as they are. **It is even more impossible to know if the origin of the**

200+ 'physical constants' precede the origin of atomic matter in the Universe or vice-versa? Or both might have evolved simultaneously together and got mutually tuned? Halit Eroglu[23] has recently derived all fundamental physical constants from a new formula **(ℏ. c = Square Root of 10)** discovered by him and so also some very interesting correlations in the quantum world. Time factor in addition to the quantized values has been shown to be responsible for the dynamics of natural constants. According to Eroglu[23] "Like all other physical quantities 'Time' is also quantized and all interactions between quantized sizes take place in accordance to quantized timing cycles". The bizarre precise tuning of the values of 200+ physical constants is believed by some to be the handy-work of an outside super-intelligent creator. But super-intelligence is inherently ingrained itself, in the structure, composition, characteristics, properties, function and behaviour of all the atoms of various kinds. There is therefore, no need for any other external super-intelligence as a creator. Even minutest change in the value of any one of these physical constants would have made the existence of the universe and conscious matter impossible. **Under the scheme of such universal material creation at the moment the Universe came into being or the proverbial 'Big-Bang' occurred, is there also a speculative possibility to assume that highly energetic, mysteriously constituted 'conscious-quantum-particulate-entity' called the 'Soul' / 'Quantum Monod' with individual characteristic identity similar to those of the atoms, were also simultaneously created from the primordial cosmic energy and manifested as living organisms only after favourable environmental / epigenetic conditions such as those on the Earth were found?** If true, then it does not rule out the presence of such 'Quantized-Potential-Primordial Souls' everywhere in the Universe and certainly their transportation on the Earth from outer space a possibility. Coupling and connecting with them from Earth is therefore only a matter of tuning and matching our inherent energy frequency and establishing a harmonic resonance. And such a possibility and capacity within human body indeed exists and has been demonstrated by several Saints and 'Rishis'[24,25,26]. Researches in the area of 'Exobiology' and 'Extra-Terrestrial-Origin of life' also confirm the creation, origin, sustenance and existence of biomolecules within the intervening medium of our Solar system and inter-galactic space. Curiously enough, all bio-molecules, like the atoms, indeed form 'Quantum Entities' with similar characteristics, for example; spin, vibrations, frequencies and electrical charge distribution along their molecular-chain-length and polar ends. Studies on quantum interactions in biological molecules conducted by researchers from the Weizmann Institute have recently shown that DNA molecules are extremely sensitive to electron spin and can discern and filter the electrons moving through them [27]. Still however, as long as the mystery about the 'primordial cosmic energy' remains scientifically unresolved so long as the mystery about the constitution and composition of 'Souls' will remain shrouded in the realm of spiritual ambiguity. Perhaps the newer experiments planned, beyond recent discovery of 'Higgs Boson– the proverbial 'GOD Particle', from the Large Hadron Collider (LHC) accelerator may reveal some deeper clues. For the first time in the history of particle accelerators and colliders, the LHC will be able to probe beyond the now well-established physics of the Standard Model. It will certainly push the theory to discover new physics and lead physicists into a realm hitherto still unknown. Having now discovered the Higgs particle, the new goal for conducting experiments with the LHC would be to tie the loose ends within the Standard Model and perhaps, this may require a new theory. For example, according to Standard Model, particles acquire and possess mass because of the effect of the Higgs force but it does not explain why different types of particles have different masses? Why a muon particle is 207 times heavier than an electron or why a top quark is so enormously massive as compared to the other quarks? Further, the Standard Model of particle physics can neither explain as to why there are three generations of elementary matter particles. Another important embarrassing question that the Standard Model of particle physics has been unable to resolve being that most of the matter present in the universe appears to consist of an unknown substance, which does not emit light and is only known through its gravitational influence on other matter. For this reason it is known as dark matter. It is believed that dark matter is composed of huge quantities of very-weekly-interacting-relic-particles that were produced in prodigious amounts soon after the Big Bang occurred and the universe came into being about 13.7 billion years ago. If this logic and reason is correct, then it is expected that this particle may spring up in experiments, any day, any time, in the Large Hadron Collider. Fundamental particles have been classified into two separate classes that display completely different behavior. One class of particles form- the constituents of matter, while the other class of particles mediate the forces that hold matter together. Matter forming particles such as the electron obey the Pauli's exclusion principle, which means that each one must be in a different wave state. And this curious property is shared by all the fundamental particles from which matter is formed and they include; protons, neutrons and the quarks. In fact it is this property that enables them to condense into matter and collectively they are known as fermions after Professor Enrico Fermi. Likewise, the particles whose exchange produces a force, such as photons behave in a completely different way because they exist in the same wave state and form a single wave (e.g. Laser). Particles that behave in this way are collectively known as bosons after the Indian physicist Professor Satyendra Nath Bose. The matter and the force-carrying particles could then be paired up, with force-carrying particle for each matter particle and *vice versa*. This is the sort of deep relationship that is believed to be lying at the heart of matter and what the physicists are exactly striving for. A unity, that leads to more profound understanding of the universe. Its discovery would represent a major step forward towards total unification of all the four forces of nature and all the particles within a single theory which has been given the name as- 'Supersymmetry'. Supersymmetry has therefore been described as- 'a symmetry between matter-forming particles, such as electrons and quarks, and force-mediating particles, such as photons, gluons and the

Higgs Boson'. And 'Supersymmetry' is believed to unite the matter and force particles together in a warm, mutual metaphorically masculine embrace of the sturdy mass particles entwined with the metaphorically feminine force-carrying particles. *(compare and contrast this scientific fact to the ancient Vedic philosophy of pairing masculine- Bramha, Vishnu and Mahesh with their feminine counterparts Saraswati, Lakshmi and Parvati respectively, described in the author's write-up on Lord Dattatreya (Figure 2) as a front-piece to this book. Further, the theoretical demand of 'supersymmetry' requiring matter-carrying particles and force-carrying particles to essentially have equal amount of electric charge on them for pairing is akin to the concept of 'Ardha-Nari-Nateshwara' equal halves of masculine Shiva and feminine Parvati in the constitution of human body* (Figure 3). If the universe is really governed by the supersymmetric laws, then each type of matter-carrying particle has to have its complementary supersymmetry force-mediating partner. Conversely, each force-mediating particle has a supersymmetric matter-carrying particle. Theoretically matter-carrying particle and force-carrying particles for supersymmetry pairing must have exactly the same amount of electric charges, but this is not the case for the particles that are currently known to physicists, therefore all the known particles cannot be paired up in this way. Therefore, if supersymmetry is indeed the symmetry of the real world, then it would imply the existence of many different new particles to be discovered in the years to come. There would be a new superpartner particle for each of the known particle. And physicists, in anticipation of their discovery in the years to come, have already provided suitable names for all such particles. Their suggested names for instance being; superpartner of photon will be known as photino, superpartners of W and Z particles will be known as Winos and Zinos, superpartner of gluon as gluinos, superpartner of Higgs is Higgsino and that of electron and quark as selectron and squark respectively. Their discovery would reveal the origin of the dark matter so abundantly distributed in the universe [28]. The tremendously ultimate and ambitious goal of theoretical physicists is to find a single theory that encompasses the whole of physics and answers all our fundamental questions about the universe and the material within it. This dream was inflamed by Albert Einstein. And the recent discovery of the 'Higgs particle' is the first greatest achievement in of the twenty first century towards this end. It indeed marks as a definitive proof that we all as conscious organisms, are really living continuously connected within a 'cosmic superconductor' [28]. Perhaps, the nature, manifestation and composition of the kind of energy involved in the constitution of that enigmatic, illusive particle what we call by the name of 'Soul' / 'Quantum Monod' /'Prana' / 'Atma' (If it ever separately exists?) may not be known today but intuitively enough, it cannot be any different from the perpetual energy-matter interactions going on in the Universe at the subtlest level.

The atomic elements in specific combinations come together under specific circumstances and conditions to form innumerable structures of various kinds only to disintegrate after specific interval of time or under specific conditions or environments into their component atoms to be recycled to form new structures of similar or dissimilar kinds. Recycling of these basic atomic material units is therefore the fundamental law and characteristic of the material world in nature [4]. Living organisms are often described as lumps of conscious matter. **And it remains to be seen if, besides their constituent material contents, Souls of all living organisms also form an integral part of the 'Recycling Nature'?** Modern science has so far no answers and even if there are answers, the question is only open to debate without freedom from bondages of religious dogmatisms, prejudices and blind beliefs in our religious 'meta-narrative' books. Moreover, just because something is scientifically difficult to prove for the time being does not make it impossible. We are aware of the history, that even celebrated scientists as Lord Kelvin and A. A. Michelson, by the end of the 19th century had emphatically declared- "all that was to be discovered has already been done so and no further developments in physical science is possible". And yet, the spectacular discoveries of radio-activity, X-Rays, electrons, protons, neutrons, relativity, uncertainty principle, De Broglie Hypothesis and wave-particle duality, planetary model for atom, concepts of electron jumps into higher electron orbits around central nucleus of atoms, multi-universes (multiverse) and quantum physics have pushed the frontiers of knowledge beyond imagination and perception of even the most celebrated scientists of the 19th century mentioned above. However, Consciousness is essential for any understanding and comprehension. Material creation, its beauty and grandeur has no value without the presence of a conscious observer. Consciousness is therefore at the centre of all creation and the Universe is essentially 'Bio-centric' and not 'Material-centric' as is generally believed. Today, new thinking, interpretations and paradigm shifts on related concepts as possible explanations are emerging in the form of 'theory of morphic or morphogenetic fields, morphic resonance and morphogenesis' proposed and pioneered by Rupert Sheldrake [9-12], 'theory of Epigenetics' by Bruce H. Lipton [29] and 'theory of Bio-Centrism' proposed by Robert Lanza [30,31]. Sir William Lawrence Bragg (NL) had once very rightly said- **"The important thing in science is not so much to obtain new facts as to discover new ways of thinking about them, because the sole purpose and aim of science is to do honour to the (inquisitive) human spirit"**.

1.6 Observed and reported cases of reincarnation / re-birth / life after-death

Considerable data has now been gathered on modern scientific logic, experimental analysis, and voluminous amount of observations and experiences collected from thousands of cases of rebirth of individuals, cutting across continents, nationalities, cultures, religious faiths and physical conditions of existence on the Earth. All these studies [5-8, 12,14], rigorously tested on the strength of statistical and regression analysis as reported, are suggesting the possibility of a common cause, purpose, process, reason and science for our repeated cyclic births, spanning several centuries and irregular time intervals in between each births.

There is apparently a common denominator in observations recorded by these individuals of case studies about experiences felt and memorized between earlier lives and rebirth. **Therefore, whether we understand or do not understand, willingly accept or unwillingly ignore, consciously subscribe to or thoughtlessly discard, we must be magnanimously open to accept the fact as scientific truth or obstinately or arrogantly refuse with a pre-conditioned mindset, there has to be but only one universal common scientific theory, law, rules and conditions that govern the existence of the entire human race and other forms of living beings on the Earth and for cycles of continued existence through births and rebirths.** If in case we assume that some form of Soul persists beyond death, it remains to be explained what particles is that soul made of, what kind and nature of known or unknown forces hold it together and how does it interact with ordinary matter? Unfortunately, nobody from the advocates for life-after-death, has tried to sit down and do the hard work of explaining how the basic physics of atoms and electrons beyond rules laid down by the Standard Model of particle physics would have to be altered or interpreted in order for this to be true or explained. Continued belief in life-after-death either requires entirely new physics and understanding on how that interacts with the familiar matter or otherwise an entirely new but innovative explanation and interpretation on the basis of the existing laws of physics. We need to attempt and arrive at some satisfactory scientific explanation than to remain perpetually ignorant and clouded in blind faith and dogmatic orthodoxy. Most essentially, we need to understand that our belief in rebirth of an individual from the historical past is factually linked only to looking for comparative similarities of the qualities of head, heart, valour and wits with someone born in the present. We seldom bother, compare or consider their physical body-structure, constitution or appearances. This essentially conveys the scientific message that it is not the physical return in rebirth of an individual from the past but the characteristics and power of the self-replicating-DNA molecule within cellular replication processes, in shaping the birth of a new individual with nearly similar or identical attributes in association with epigenetic environment during conception, gestation to birth. We therefore need only to seek a convincing scientific explanation for transfer of memory and information from one generation to the other than to pursue the impossible belief or reality of anyone coming to rebirth after death [18]. It is, in fact a purely accidental, near exact resemblance of an individual in qualities of head, heart, mind, thoughts and deeds with someone who had lived in the historical past and whose memories are preserved in our documentary records that prompts us to believe in his / her cyclic rebirth. In the absence of any memory or such documented record about any person who had lived in the past, belief in rebirth loses all its consideration, relevance and significance. Moharir [18] has very strongly argued against the possibility of the whole concept of rebirth. However, the only scientifically justifiable truth being the possible birth of a new individual resembling in characteristics with someone who had displayed similar traits in the past. And such individual characteristic traits are repeatedly reproduced in human beings over specific intervals of time from specific combinations and interaction of self-replicating genes (DNA) during cellular replication processes and cyclic environmental conditions (terrestrial and cosmic both inclusive). **Therefore physical return in rebirth of individuals after death is just not possible. It is only the repeat cyclic emergence of the characteristic traits and attributes in new individuals arising from the routine manifestation of the self-replicating DNA molecules and combination of millions of encoded proteins synthesized by them in response to the stimulus from the surrounding environment.**

Renowned Biologist Professor Richard Dawkins also mentions in his celebrated book- 'The Selfish Gene' [32] and it is worth quoting here - "Individuals are not stable things, they are fleeting. Chromosomes (Genes) too are shuffled into oblivion, like hands of cards soon after they are dealt. But the cards themselves survive the shuffling. The cards are the genes. The genes are not destroyed by crossing-over in shuffling, they merely change partners and march on. Of course they march on. That is their business. They are the replicators and we are their survival machines. When we have served our purpose we are cast aside. But the genes are denizens of geological time: Genes are forever." And – "For more than three thousand million years, DNA has been the only replicator worth talking about in the world. But this does not necessarily hold these monopoly rights for all time. Whenever conditions arise in which a new kind of replicator can make copies of itself, the new replicators will tend to takeover, and start a new kind of evolution of their own".

1.7 Vedic philosophy about birth, death and reincarnation / rebirth / life-after-death

The earliest references to the concept and practical truth about birth, death and rebirth in human beings comes from the Vedic scriptures and Vedic civilization that flourished in ancient India some 25,000 years BC [1-3, 33-35]. The first entry and final exit of what is called as the prana or the 'soul' from the body were synonymous with life and death. The Indian concepts of breath energy- prana – have predated and indeed inspired those originating from Europe and China. Hindus believe that in addition to the physical body, there is an astral body connected to the physical body by means of a thread, which is severed at death. The civilization at Vedic time was homogenously apolitical and not divided between multitude of organized religious groups, factions and faiths as it is now in the twenty first century. The emphatic statement on the truth about rebirth is found in the words of Shrikrishna, delivered on the battlefield of Kurukshetra on 16 th October 5561 BC [1] *(Date corresponding to Indian calendar system prevalent, practiced and recorded in verses in the 'Shrimad Bhagwad Gita' and interpolated back in Gregorian Calendar for easy comprehension of the elapsed time span by Dr. P. V. Vartak).* Here, Shrikrishna clearly states about hundreds of cycles of death and rebirth lived by everyone present on the battle field, with the only difference that whereas everyone else has forgotten about their repeated past lives between deaths and rebirths, Shrikrishna distinctly remembers (realizes or understands) his own births. Thousands of years after Shrikrishna, it was Gautam Buddha who has been known to have distinctly remembered all his past births and deaths which include **357** lives as a human beings, **66** as Gods and **123** as animals, indicating thereby the factual possibility of trans-migration of soul from human to 'godly angelic' individuals to the animal life forms in between successive births. **Surprisingly however, there is neither mention nor description of the sequential order of the births and rebirths of Gautam Buddha.** In both these cases, it is impossible to believe that both Shrikrishna and Gautam Buddha should have factually remembered their individual identity all through the cycles of their births, deaths and rebirths. **It seems more probable, reasonable, logical and scientifically consistent to believe that both Shrikrishna and Gautam Buddha, being knowledgeable about Vedic philosophy and Upanishads (Buddhism as a religion was not even born until Buddha himself lived his life), were in fact, citing their own lives, deaths and rebirths as metaphoric examples in explaining the cardinal principle of perpetually cyclic nature of material creation, existence and destruction going on in the universe and perhaps not of the individuals or their enigmatic Souls.** And this cycle is common to both the inanimate and animate matter and nothing more. It is perhaps our enamoured love, affection, appreciation and emotional attachment to the personalities, qualities and teachings of both Shrikrishna and Gautam Buddha individually, that have blind-folded ourselves to overlook the factual scientific truth in their statements and mistakenly assume them to being endowed with super-natural powers. Both, Shrikrishna and Gautam Buddha were human beings like any other individual. Shrikrishna was bestowed and invoked with God-hood more than 2500 years after his death as per records mentioned by Dr. P. V. Vartak [3], and Gautam Buddha, during his own life time, had clearly emphasized that he was neither a GOD nor a messenger of a GOD. **His enlightenment was not the result of a supernatural prowess, power, process or agency, but rather the result of close and minute attention** he paid to the nature of the human mind which could be rediscovered by anyone for himself. On the contrary, Buddhism, defined, professed and practiced long after Buddha himself was gone, denies the concept of an eternal, individualized Soul but does include some ideas resembling Soul such as 'skandas', which carry <u>memories</u> of a person's karma into future lives, and advanced practitioner of Buddhism can attain the 'Rainbow body', to enable him to exist beyond his physical body.

1.8 Religious philosophies are based on third-person accounts

It is a historical fact that stories about the life, work and philosophy of both Shrikrishna and Gautam Buddha and also in respect of Jesus Christ, Prophet Mohammad, Lord Mahavir and Guru Nanak were written, compiled, edited or interpreted by their followers long after they were gone. Neither of them had told nor even written their own biographies. Information about all of them has descended down to us from the records written by third persons, either contemporary or otherwise. The 'Mahabharata' itself has seen three editions before coming into the present form from originally containing 8,800 verses written by Ved Vyasa to 24,000 verses in the version edited by Rishi Vaishampayan and finally to 100,000 verses in the version compiled and edited by Rishi Sauti, sequentially within a span of about one thousand years from Ved Vyas [32]. **Therefore, there appears to be something fundamentally wrong or quite possibly a distortion in communication and in understanding the messages of both, Shrikrishna and Gautam Buddha about the factual reality or mystery of remembering their own births and rebirths.** Even in the case of Shri Ram in the epic 'Ramayana', he has been essentially described as an ordinary human being all through the text, except a brief mention to his (Ram's) being an incarnation in the 'Bal-Kaand' and 'Sunder-Kaand' chapters.

The very fact that psychic, intuitive, spiritual or telepathic communication over long distances can be established with even pet or wild animals by animal-communicators today, suggests that there exists a common subtle bond between all life forms because consciousness within plants, human beings and all other forms of animate life forms is incredibly similar / identical (Daniel Chamovitz, Director, Manna Center for Plant Sciences, Tel Aviv University, Israel, and Rupert Sheldrake (2011)- "Dogs know When their Owners are Coming Home, and other Unexplained Powers of Animals' Three River Press). Both Shrikrishna and Gautam Buddha clearly stand out as the only human beings who understood the true nature of the cyclic universe. No wonder, they both are considered by the Hindus as the re-incarnations of Lord Vishnu, the Omni-present-potential cosmic consciousness / energy or force of nature that sustains and recycles material creation. Therefore, there appears to be some justification for a thorough scientific investigation about why should memory about past births, even in very few reported cases could be retained whereas in majority of other individuals gets totally absent or lost?

1.9 Modern concept of atoms and molecules: Their structures, combinations and functions

The earliest references to the concepts of atoms and molecules can apparently be found in the Mahabharata **(5561 BC)** with mention of the use of the atomic weapon like devices called as the 'Bramhastra' in this war. This looks possibly so, because the factual description of the situation that arose after the detonation of 'Bramhastra' corresponds ditto parallel with the description recorded in the modern history after the first two atomic nuclear fission bombs were dropped on the cities of Hiroshima and Nagasaki in Japan during the World War-II. There is no description about how the Sages and 'Rishis' of the Vedic times came to arrive at the concepts of atom and molecules described in Sanskrit as *'Anuu'* and *'Parmanuu'* respectively but they were certainly aware of this reality. The very fact that these words have been mentioned in the Vedic literature, justify that the Vedic Rishies were not only knowledgeable about atoms and molecules but they were even widely using the atomic or molecular processes of electroplating for depositing silver and gold over base metals [33,34]. Science, technology and industry was indeed a part of the Vedic culture [37].

The idea of atoms constituting the material world originated in antiquity. Leucippus and Epicurus the Greek philosophers were already talking about all matter being made of infinity of infinitely small particles in eternal motion. Democritus Abdera, another Greek philosopher (about 500 B.C.) in an eloquent statement on atomic hypothesis wrote: "By convention sour, by convention sweet, by convention coloured; in reality, nothing but Atoms and the void." It was the great English chemist John Dalton who not only reiterated the atomic concept in 1808 but also showed that atoms of dissimilar elements combine in some fixed proportions. The atoms of about 118 kinds of similar or dissimilar elements present in nature, in combinations enter into the composition of all known composite substances. The atoms or molecules can only vibrate, without displacement like the stems of wheat or maize crop plants bending before the wind but without changing their places. Further developments in the modern theory of atomic structure of matter had made it very clear that the size of the atoms, if they existed, would be extremely small to be perceived directly by our senses or even seen under the most powerful microscope. To confirm the physical reality of the existence of atoms, an ingenious idea was adopted to assume or theorize that atoms indeed existed and then develop some logical experiments based on this assumption in anticipation of some perceptible consequences. Any matching of observed consequences in accordance with assumptions would mean an indirect confirmation for the existence of atoms. Several experiments conducted by Bernoulli, James Clark Maxwell, Ludwig Boltzmann, Robert Boyle, Jacques Cesar Charles and finally Albert Einstein unequivocally demonstrated that atoms indeed exist. Robert Brown demonstrated and recognized the perpetual motion of pollen grains suspended in water, the 'Brownian Motion' to be caused by the pushing thrusts exerted on the pollen grains by continually dynamic molecules of water made of two hydrogen atoms joined together to one oxygen atom. Albert Einstein developed a mathematical theory to explain the Brownian motion and its theoretical predictions were not only confirmed by Jean-Baptiste Perrin but he even calculated the size of atoms to be of the order of a billionth part of a metre in diameter. It was however left to Sir J. J. Thomson, Ernest Rutherford, Niels Bohr and several others to fully describe how an atom looks like and functions. Perhaps the best possible examples of the power of formulation of logical conceptual theories are the law of periodic table of elements discovered by Dmitri I. Mendeleev, who predicted existence and properties of new elements long before they were physically discovered in nature and more recently, the theoretical prediction of the existence of an elementary particle- 'The Higgs Boson' also nicknamed as 'The GOD Particle' that provides mass to energy, by Peter Higgs almost fifty years before it was experimentally discovered at the CERN (European Centre for Nuclear Research, Geneva) in 2012-2013. The mechanisms involved in these theoretical models do not make it a precondition to physically experience observations through our five senses before we understand and accept them as has been imprinted in our minds by the classical Newtonian physics. For example, look at the new concept of an electron jumping instantaneously from one orbit shell around nucleus to another without physically moving across the space between the consecutive shells. Here, electrons just disappear from one orbit shell and reappear in the other. This disappearance and re-appearance of electron is akin to its death in one orbit shell and rebirth in the other. Alternately, disappearing from one universe and reappearing into another. Mechanisms and explanation of such phenomena are not only beyond our imagination but can only be explained on the basis of quantum mechanics and not by classical physics. Whereas classical Newtonian physics stood for absolute physical quantities and their absolute measurements, modern physics believes in the impossibility of absolute quantities and their measurements which are not only relative but represent only the probabilities of their being a reality.

1.10 Quanta and Quantum Particles

The discovery of the atom *(irrespective of its 118 different elemental kinds)* marks the landmark departure from the classical physical science. Atoms consist of over 99.9% empty space with over 99.9% of their masses being concentrated within a minutest region at the centre, called the nucleus, compared to the size of the atoms. The nuclei of atoms were discovered to be charged electrically positive and nuclear physicists pictured the atom as a miniature solar system with distribution of negatively charged electrons around the nucleus to make the atom as electrically neutral. This theoretical picture defied classical Newtonian laws of motion and new laws had to be discovered to explain the perpetual motion of electrons without gradually losing their energy and spirally colliding into the nucleus leading to its annihilation or something to that effect. Nothing like this happens in reality and to explain the motion of electrons around the nuclei of atoms, Niels Bohr adopted the concept described by Max Planck in that a body absorbs or emits energy in the form of radiation, not continuously but discontinuously in integral multiples of a definite amount of packets called quantum. The magnitude of the quantum depends on the vibration frequency of the oscillator i.e. electron. If ν is the frequency of vibration the quantum Q of energy is given by $Q = \hbar.\nu$ where $\hbar$ is the Planck's universal constant. Energy can be taken up or given out in such quanta only. **The role of electrons is primordial in that it is electrons which give a substance most of its physical and chemical properties and it is their number which determines the physical identity of the elemental atom i.e. whether it is hydrogen, iron or uranium. Chemical combinations are always brought about when electrons are either shared or exchanged between two or more interacting atoms to form structures** [4]. Both atoms and molecules (depending on the number of atoms involved in combination to form a molecule) constitute quantum particles in perpetual state of vibration with characteristic frequencies and wavelengths. The diameters of the atoms are of the order of a ten millionth of a millimeter and that of the least voluminous molecules measure 2-3 times as much[4]. The individual molecules routinely encountered in organic (or biological chemistry) assume much larger sizes and can be easily visualized under powerful electron or atomic force microscopes. In molecules of similar and dissimilar atoms, regions of varying electron density are usually found around atoms and their bonds. The electron density distribution is therefore a measure of the probability of an electron being present at a specific location along the molecular length.

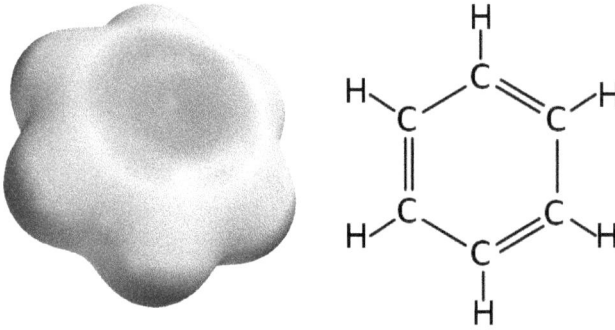

Figure 4. Here is an example of an electrostatic potential map of benzene molecule (Left) and its corresponding two dimensional molecular structures of six carbon atoms forming a hexagonal ring (Right) Reproduced with apology from Wikipedia.

A look at the electron density map or the structural formula of a molecule is enough to suggest to a chemist, which regions are electron-rich and so vulnerable to electrophilic attack and which are more likely to attract nucleophilic reagents, thereby permitting calculation of the external electrostatic potential and the interaction energy between molecules or between parts of the same molecule.

Recently in July 2019, a group of researchers from the IBM Research Zurich (www.sciencealert.com dated 07/15/2019) photographed four different types of molecules namely; azobenzene, pentacene, tetracynaoquinodimethane (TCNQ) and prophine, significantly changing in their structural conformation on the application of electric charge. They used the most advanced Atomic Force Microscopy technique to record with unprecedented resolution, the structural changes of individual molecules upon charging. The researchers imaged all the four molecules under two or more of the following four different states of charging; positive (minus one electron), neutral (the same number of protons and electrons), negative (plus one electron) and double negative (plus two electrons). All four molecules reacted differently to the changes in electric charge. These findings will have a serious impact on our understanding of how electric charge alters structure and function of molecules, which are vital in so many ways, such as photo-conversion and energy transport in living organisms and leading to profound applications in correcting physiological imbalances, genetic defects and several other kinds of disorders linked to erratic functioning of organs or behavior of human beings. These observations also convey the fact that electric charges are at the base of all structural formations in the universe or alternately, electric charges drive the universe.

The three great themes which emerged in the 20th Century- the atom, the computer and the gene, have revolutionized science and changed the human mindset. Further, Werner Heisenberg's uncertainty principle, Albert Einstein's theory of relativity, Erwin Schrodinger's wave mechanics *(Quantum Mechanics)* and the work of Paul Andre Maurice Dirac and Richard Feynman laid the foundations of quantum physics and likewise, elucidation of the structure and function of the DNA (gene) by James D. Watson and F. H. C. Crick, that of the molecular biology and molecular genetics.

1.11 What is Life?

'Functional emergence with evolution' and 'vitalism', are the two main-stream concepts which have dominated scientific thoughts about characterization and nature of all living systems. Whereas, functionalism characterizes life by its self-organizational and self-replicating arrangements leading to purposeful functions and behaviour, the proponents of 'artificial life' consider many non-biological systems such as, self-organizing computer programs with life-like functions to be also alive. If flow of controlled amount of quantized electric charge on electrons, in the form of a sequential computer program can replicate life-like functions and behavior, why not the actual flow of electric charge through body systems (which are essentially electrical in nature, mediated by the flow of atomic ions) of all living organisms and their control over the operational function and behavior of the organisms be primarily attributed to electric charge rather than to the hypothetical, abstract, illusive and enigmatic concept of the Soul? [4, 21, 37, 38]. Electricity is both a fundamental and universal natural entity. It consists of positive and negatively charged particles that mutually exhibit attractions and repulsions. Such attractions and repulsions manifest themselves into movement of these charged particles to setup and establish flow of electric currents [29, 37-40]. This form of energy plays a critical role in the proper function of the metabolism of our body and its organs. The elements in our bodies, like sodium, potassium, calcium and magnesium, have a specific electric charge. Almost all of our cells use these charged element atoms, called ions, to generate electricity. Electrical activity in our body is initiated by the ions and their movements through millions of ion channels [29, 37, 41, 42]. An ion is an atom or a group of atoms (molecules) carrying an electric charge by virtue of having gained or lost one or more valence electrons. Valence electrons are those that move in the outermost ring of electrons orbiting around the nuclei of the atoms. Ions may exist in solid, liquid or gaseous environments. Ionic solid chemical compounds are generally called as salts and the ions existing in liquid state as the electrolytes. Electrolytes in solutions conduct electric currents and are decomposed by electric currents. The process of such decomposition of electrolytes in solutions is known as electrolysis. Electrolytes play an essential role in the functioning of our bodies. Cells create electrical energy when ions move from within the cells to solutions outside the cell membranes. Thus all our body activities such as thinking, emotional responses, eating, listening, speaking, muscular movements, glandular secretions, digestion, excretions, temperature regulation and every bodily action is performed only as a result of the movement of ions or electrically charged molecules [43]. These little known but crucially important movements of ionic bio-molecules (proteins / ion channels) found in every cell of our body and in those of all living organisms on earth regulate lives of all bio-organisms from the moment of conception to their last breath. Ion channels are truly the 'spark of life' for they govern every aspect of our life and behavior [43,44]. From the lashing of the sperm's tail to sexual attraction, the beating of our hearts, the craving for coffee, ice cream or chocolate, and the feel of the warmth from sun on our skin - everything is underpinned by ion-channel activity [43-45]. In case of the mechanism by which the Venus flytrap feels the presence of its prey is identically similar to the way we feel a crawling fly on our person. Touch receptors in our skin sense the insect and activate an electrical signal that pass along our sensory nerves to the brain. The brain registers the signal and interprets the presence of fly and stimulates reaction through muscular responses. Similarly, when the insect rubs against the hairs of the Venus flytrap plant (Pitcher Plant), it induces an electrical signal that radiates throughout the leaves. As a result the ion channels in the leaf cell membrane are activated to suddenly shut the fly trap in less than one tenth of a second to catch the insect as its prey.

Figure 5: **Venus flytrap** –*dionaea muscipula.*

Thus, ions play an important role in the bodies of all living organisms. Calcium, Potassium, Sodium, Magnesium, Chloride and Copper ions participate in the body's electrical events [45]. Potassium is the major positive ion inside the cells and Sodium in the fluids outside the cells. Ionic Chloride is the most abundant negative ion. **Any imbalance of these ions in the bodies of organisms or inhibition of Sodium ion transport across cell membranes leads to dysfunction in the conduction of electrical messages. Such dysfunction produces disturbances and the loss of ability to maintain stable internal conditions. No surprise, an impaired functioning of ion channels is responsible for many human, plant and animal diseases. Ion channels are the gate-keepers of the cells and their opening and closing is controlled by intra- and extra- cellular chemicals, mechanical stress, thermodynamic fluctuations or changes in the voltage difference across cell membranes** [39-41]. Farm animals such as pigs that suddenly shiver themselves to death, a herd of goats that falls over when suddenly startled or threatened, people with cystic fibrosis, epilepsy, heart arrhythmias and migraine-

are all the victims of a factual dysfunction of their ion channels [21]. Historically, work done by some of the greatest researchers such as Allesandro Volta, Humphry Davy, Michael Faraday, Andre-Marie Ampere, James Clerk Maxwell and several others conclusively demonstrated that there is essentially no difference between bio-energy and electricity that runs through voltaic pile with further realization and conviction that psychic or bio-energy activities and all aspects of body metabolisms from the functioning of various glands, organs, brain and heart arise from the electrical activity of over thirty billion cells in human body. Not only this, but electricity is also the power behind all our senses and emotions. Bio-energy is indeed real and physically based phenomena [28].

Dick Frans Swaab [19] an internationally known researcher on human brain, in his very celebrated book clearly mentions- "I have yet to hear a good argument against my simple conclusion that the 'mind' is the product of the activity of our hundred billion brain cells and the 'soul' merely a misconception. The universality of the notion of a 'soul' seems merely to spring from mankind's fear of death, the longing to see the dear departed once again, and the misplaced, arrogant idea that we are so important that something must remain of us after death. The product of the interaction of all these billions of neuron cells is what we call 'mind'. Just as kidneys produce urine, the brain produces mind, as Jacob Moleschott (1882-1893) so immutably put it. But now we know what this process actually entails; electrical activity, the release of chemical messengers, changes in cell contacts and alterations in the activity of nerve cells. Brain scans are used not only to trace diseases of the brain but also to show which areas light up during different activities, so that we know which parts we use to read, think, calculate, listen to music, have religious experiences, fall in love, or become sexually excited. By observing the changing patterns of the brain, we can train it to function differently. Malfunction in this efficient information processing machine cause psychiatric and neurological disorders. Paradoxically, these disorders tell us much more about the way in which the brain normally functions".

And similarly, Dr. Carlo Rovelli, an Italian Theoretical Physicist (in his book-Seven Brief Lessons on Physics, 2014, p.91) writes- "We have a hundred billion neurons in our brains, as many as there are stars in a galaxy, with an even more astronomical number of links and potential combinations through which they can interact. We are not conscious of all of this. 'We' are the process formed by this entire intricacy, not just by the little of it of which we are conscious. The 'I' who decides is the same 'I' which is formed from reflections upon itself; through self-representations in the world; from understanding itself as a variable point of view placed in the context of the world; from that impressive structure that processes information and constructs representations which is our brain. When we have the feeling that 'it is I' who decides we could not be more correct, who else? I am my body and what happens in my brain and heart, with their immense and inextricable complexity." Therefore, it is the human brain, which because of the intensive electrical activity going on in its network of billions of neuron cells, essentially provides a man / woman, his / her personal identity 'I' and a feeling of Conscious 'Self-Awareness'. Kenneth Nealson, from the University of Southern California, Los Angeles emphatically says-"Life is a flow of electrons. You eat sugars that have excess electrons, and when you breathe oxygen that willingly takes them. Our cells break down the sugars, and the electrons flow through them in a complex set of biochemical reactions until they are passed on to electron-hungry oxygen. Life is very clever. It figures out how to suck electrons out of everything we eat and keep them under control. In almost all living things, the body packages the electrons up into molecules that can safely carry them through the cells until they are dumped on to oxygen. Electrons must flow in order for energy to be gained. This is why when someone suffocates another person they are dead within minutes. You have stopped the supply of oxygen, so that the electrons can no longer flow".

In a way, perhaps we may be failing to recognize electric charge to be the *de-facto* 'Soul' which is considered and held responsible for the function and behavior of all living organisms.

Therefore, it is pertinent to reason, argue and ponder- If our ancient 'concept of Soul' may appear to be a religious dogma or a prejudiced obsession descended down to us through thousands of years of human civilizations? Has this dogmatic concept by any chance prevented us from thinking objectively and taking a truly scientific look at the 'Soul' beyond reasons already discussed above? Incidentally, all the attributes of soul, described since thousands of years in that the soul being; deathless, decay-less, timeless, causeless, space-less, and being the source and substratum for the bodies of all living organisms, their mind and the whole creation in the universe, are ditto identical with the experimentally established properties of electrons, the common constituent of all matter.

The term 'Emergence' implies a hierarchical organization, built from simple components at lower levels with life arising from complex interactions within and between the constituent component parts. 'Life', therefore is believed to emerge from complex interactions between atoms, ions and polar or non-polar bio-molecules made-up of atoms. The bio-molecules on the other hand are more complex and complicated. Their organization into structures of biological systems, interactions, properties, functions and behavior are governed by the nature, position and properties of various types of atoms or group of atoms and their movements within and across biological systems, mediated through the specific and specialized ion channels. Such functional and emergent approaches, based on reductionism are being frequently used these days in molecular biology. On the other hand, 'Vitalism' the other main-stream, based on electromagnetism or essentially on imaginary forces from outside the known realm of science, stands discarded for good with the advent of quantum mechanics. **Erwin Schrodinger, the founder of quantum mechanics suggested in 1944, that the essential framework of life is engrained in 'aperiodic lattices' and all living systems are fundamentally quantized.** This description is relevant for both DNA and RNA, the cytoskeletal protein assemblies, microtubules and actin-gels that criss-cross the entire cell matrix. With recent evidence of bio-molecules being also capable of harnessing ambient heat and energy to promote their functional quantum states instead of causing de-coherence, the non-local quantum correlations amongst the bio-molecules are considered to be responsible for unified inherent behaviours of living systems (Roger Penrose). It is a considered general opinion of all celebrated scientists since Erwin Schrodinger that life is related to organized quantum processes in π electron resonance clouds within bio-molecules. And biology perhaps evolved initially from simple oil-water interfaces and adopted to utilize cooperative quantum processes to its best advantage with minimum expenditure of energy.

Three theories are currently in vogue regarding the origin of life. One assumes an involvement of a 'Creator', the second involves a sudden spontaneous chemical activity leading to formation of self replicating bio-molecules and the third assumes seeding of the earth from extra-terrestrial (Exobiology) sources such as meteorites, comets and asteroids. However, even such explanations still need to explain the origin of life in conditions of extra-terrestrial space before transportation to earth for manifestation and proliferation. Further, bio-molecules such as simple peptides, sugars, lipids and nucleic acids have been observed to be formed spontaneously in marine salt water or near geo-thermal vents (Geysers), volcanoes and in clay minerals. What is mysterious is their incorporation, culmination, evolution and adaptation into structural organelles and their coalescence to become the cooperating parts of an integrated biological cell as the basic units of all life-forms, irrespective of origin from soil, plant, animal or aquatic source. All these appear to suggest 'intelligent design' and obviously to 'Creationism'. But according to Roger Penrose, intelligent design simply reflects the type of Platonic *(harmless or ineffectual)* information embedded in the Planck scale. **And if this is true; then it implies that all living systems are perpetually in constant touch with some deeper reality of the universe through quantum states.** Even Swami Satyanand Saraswati [26] observes that- "research on the nature of available energies in the universe indicate that consciousness may be independent from the body of organisms, suggesting thereby, that all living organisms may be integrally connected to the universal consciousness". And such a conclusion has also been argued earlier in this book during discussion on supersymmetry. However, this does not mean that all quantum information devices must also be 'alive'. Only organic molecules and cytoskeletal protein lattices may be endowed with inherent flexibility to harness ambient energy for quantum coherent states to interact and adjust with the Planck scale through quantum gravity processes and use photons as phase-ordered matter. But since all animate and inanimate material world is built from atoms, the above argument implies that what we call 'conscious life' may be a special property endowed to only restricted kind of atoms such as Carbon, Hydrogen (proton), Nitrogen, Calcium, Sodium, Sulphur, Magnesium, Phosphorus, Potassium and Chlorine and to molecules built from a combination of these atoms. These are the only few elements particularly, carbon, sodium, potassium and hydrogen that uniformly and predominantly go into the structural makeup and in functional operation of various body organs of all living organisms from soil, land, plant, insect, bird or aquatic origin and each one working under command (or regulated by) of its conscious enigmatic entity called the 'Soul'. Just as a house under construction does not spontaneously emerge from a pile of bricks, similarly there is nothing conscious about an electron required to emerge as consciousness from a pile of atoms put together. Most of the piles of atoms do not produce anything. They process no information and do not generate any output. Still, however, some configurations of atoms do indeed process information and generate output and are labeled as 'conscious'. And yet, it does not qualify as an emergent property as does the 'houseness' of a house that emerges from bricks, the basic building block for a house. This appears to set consciousness differently apart from electric charge on electron, proton or atomic ions. Whereas, a quantum of electric charge can be measured, a quantum of consciousness cannot be assayed so. Alternately, a certain amount of electric charge can always be expressed as a multiple of the quantum of charge on an electron but consciousness cannot similarly be divided to the level of an electron. This is because, whereas electric charge is a physical quantity, consciousness is merely an attribute, a property that arises as a result of the combinations and permutations of connecting various building blocks from a huge 'body-organism' space. It is an arbitrary definition and an arbitrary attribute of a specific association and group of atoms. It would be therefore be worthwhile to examine from such a specific angle, the composition and sequential arrangement of atoms in adenine, thymine, cytosine and guanine (A, T, C and G) groups of molecules that make the composition of the DNA, program the syntheses of proteins, initiate and sustain metabolism and functional activities of various organs at free will to generate what is called "consciousness".

1.12 What is a 'Soul'?

The soul, since antiquity, has been associated with consciousness and freedom of all life forms that exist on Earth. All religions that have flourished and perished and those still existing on earth have propounded notions of 'Soul'. Soul and body together form one unique combination of nature. Soul as an immaterial spirit is believed to be the intelligence or the so called consciousness itself. Two kinds of souls viz., the individual soul or Jivatman or the human soul, and the Supreme Soul called Paramatman, which is universal. Adi Shankaracharya was emphatic when he said that Bramha alone is real, the rest of the world is unreal, and the individual soul is nothing but Bramha. The Jivataman is merely an individual refection of the same universal Parmatman. Therefore, finer divisions between Bramha and Parabramha or Atman or Jeevatman seem unnecessary and superfluous. It is as good as saying that electric current flowing from a powerhouse is electric current but when it passes through a Table fan, it is Table fan current when both are same and identical. These various terms might have cropped up during the evolution of a formative philosophical thought but in the science and technology oriented twenty first century, all these ancient terms need to be rationalized for their uniform perception and understanding.

Everyone speaks about the Soul but rarely has anyone attempted to dare, ponder and describe what exactly it is and what is its structure and configuration from the point of modern scientific basis. Traditionally, soul is believed to be beyond all sounds, all sights, all tastes, all touch, without forms and attributes, beyond nature, beyond three bodies and five sheaths (Panch-Koshas), it is infinite and unchanging, self luminous and free from birth and death. The individual soul- Jivatman, manifesting within human body is considered to be 'finite and impure' for obvious reasons. Unlike Paramatma, as a manifestation of infinite pure universal energy, the Jivatma has power, limited to its use in the working of various organs and maintain the respiratory, digestive and excretory systems of any living organism for survival as an individual unit. Further, the supreme soul, Paramatma is described to be self-conscious, self-aware, self-delight, self-knowledge, self-existent, self-luminous and illuminates everything else. Therefore, it is called the 'Chaitanya' the prime mover energy of all creation.

Despite tremendous developments in science and technology and increased resolving power of our instrumental detection techniques, Soul, as a hidden illusive entity continues to remain the most profound enigma of our life. Our knowledge about Soul continues to be vague and yet, we blindly admit that our Soul identifies who we are. **Each and every Soul is believed to be an individual and an immortal entity created by nature. It is still not clear if it is the will of the Soul that propels a body from birth to the end of its life or it is the capacity and limitation of the developed body-system that restricts the "resident time" for the Soul within itself?** However, experience suggests that when a body-system gets incapacitated (short circuited) to maintain flow of electric charge current to every organ parts in a holistic way, the immortal Soul exits it. This is why; naturally incapacitated bodies kept on external life-support remain conscious and alive to some extent or as long as the external support is continued. In a spectacular incident, reported in the newspapers recently, a premature but healthy baby was delivered by a fifteen weeks pregnant brain-dead mother who suffered a stroke and had been maintained on life-support system by the doctors in Budapest in Hungary to save the life of her baby. The baby was born alive and healthy through a cesarean operation at 27 week maturity and weighed 1.4 Kg. **It is very clear from this example that the brain of the mother had nothing to do with the development of the fetus and the baby was either developing independently and guided by its own Soul or by the Soul of its mother that did not reside in her brain but elsewhere. The external life-support system merely kept ion-channels in the bodies of both the mother and developing fetus in active functioning condition.**

A majority of people, in general, think of Soul to be a blob of immaterial spirit energy that persists after death, and this sort of substance in their mind, resides near our brain but drives around our body. **The only entity that actually moves around our entire body-system consisting of billions of individual cells constituting various organs is the electric charge and ionic current.** Vedas and Upanishads describe the Soul to be residing in the heart of the human body. This seems to be logical in that it is indeed the heart that continually distributes and circulates oxygen, the principal currency for exchange of electric charge and generator of active ion-channels in the body. This is a function analogous and similar to that of artificial life-supporting systems. The purpose of both is to supply oxygen to the body through lungs. Any limitations in the supply of oxygen lead to insufficient generation of ions and consequently feeble ionic currents to maintain all organs of multi-cellular body optimally functional. Here again, it is the essential role of electric charge that is underlined in generating consciousness. But what is that thing which not only generates but perpetually sustains the electric charge itself? Halit Eroglu [23] in his recent book maintains that the universe consists of simple components. An analog clock also consists of simple components such as gears, screws etc. Only the interaction of these basic components according to a specific system brings the clock to running state. In the universe too, it is the interaction of individual components that make the "clockwork" universe running. The space in the universe, and so also the vacuum in its smallest dimensions, according to Eroglu [23], consists of unified densely interconnected spheres with a strictly periodic structure called the "space-balls". The "space-balls" are magnetic monopoles and their elementary energy force content shows off itself in the form of attraction to pull each others. All physical phenomena are the consequences of the primal magnetism in the magnetic monopoles- the 'space-balls'. The electric charge, mass and the basic components of matter, the atoms, stars, etc. arise from the interactions between these 'space-balls' according to the following scheme;

(Space-Ball) Magnetism > Charge >Mass > Particles > Atoms > Stars

i.e. magnetism causes emergence of electric charges and these generate mass, which then form particles that accumulate into atoms and atoms in turn produce all macroscopic bodies and celestial objects in the universe.

Magnetism in 'space-balls' is a hidden power which forms the elemental force in the universe and the entire universe is built-up electromagnetically. Therefore, electrodynamics and electromagnetic interactions have their origin in the quantized magnetism. The effects of the elemental magnetism become apparent from the transport of charge. According to Eroglu [23], magnetism is the cause of electrodynamics and it brings out the charges as an effect and not the other way round. Physical calculations do not change by this order but provide better understanding of the universe with different perspective and new insights. So far, magnetic monopoles have not been detected and it is not possible to directly observe them because they themselves show no observable physical events. All physical events actually emerge from the interactions of dipoles which are formed by external influences. Halit Eroglu's explanation [23] appears consistent to the discussion developed and given above in this paper. It therefore appears to suggest that physics and physical laws concerning creation, accumulation and interactions of magnetic monopoles in the space vacuum has something to do with the origin or the identity of what we call as the 'Soul'. And since magnetic monopoles represent the elementary, primordial, all-pervading form of energy in the universe from which every other matter is created, it connects very well as the common thread with the origin and function of all living creatures on the earth. Whatever may be the truth, the questions that still remain un-answered being: what form does that soul energy take, what is its ultimate origin, constitution, nature, and location inside the body of the organism and how does it interact with other ordinary atoms? It is also not clearly known whether it is the same individual 'soul' that takes residence within body from the moment of birth / conception to the last breath at death with its known identity as 'self' or 'Me'. If it is the same soul that remains resident in the body from birth to death, how then does it loose its identity for example; when ridden with alzheimer's disease? Does the root cause for alzheimer's disease change the very identity of what we call 'soul'? Truly speaking, it is the people around us and in family, or our parents and the society in general who maintain and keep reminding us about our identity of being Mr X or Mr Y. Imagine, how a child born in the wild and somehow surviving alone after his birth will ever know his identity except realizing that he is only a conscious creature. Just as all living creatures on earth remain continually connected to the Oxygen reservoir of atmosphere from the moment of birth to the last breath, **there is therefore a reason to believe that we (as an individual soul) continually remain in touch with universal consciousness (energy / force) from the moment of birth to death, through a subtle unknown mechanism ingrained within our body-systems. The 'Soul' taking a permanent residence within the body for a life-time appears to be a pleasant likable myth.** Here, the role of subtle electrical conduits, the millions of ion-channels (In the language of modern biology) OR the conduits *(Nadi)* identified and known since millenniums in India for circulation of consciousness in our bodies, known as 'Ida', 'Pingala' and 'Sushumna' and the power grids, called the 'Chakras' for maintaining a continuous connection for functions of various body organs under their control besides regulating the flood of universal consciousness within cells and organs of body-systems appears to be very rational. The subtle energy of body is believed to have both physical and psychic properties and its most intense form is represented by the Vedic concept of serpent 'Kundalini' which normally remains dormant in each and every individual [26]. This concept of continuous connection can be easily understood when I say- "my house has running water for 24 hours". Here, it does not mean that the same quantity or amount of water stays in my house for all 24 hours but only that my house is connected to an unlimited source or a reservoir, knowing well that I am using different water every time I open tap in my house. Still however, the statement also qualifies that water stays in my house for all 24 hours in a day. Consciousness, likewise also stays in our bodies through continual connection to its universal source from the moment of birth or conception to the last breath. **A quantum entity called the 'Soul', taking a permanent residence in the body therefore appears to be a very narrow and selfish interpretation and an antique deception.**

1.13 Kundalini and human consciousness

Besides, Soul and Rebirth, the other profound concepts from the Indian philosophy have been the 'Kundalini' and the 'Chakras' which are believed to be intimately interconnected. Kundalini known as the sleeping dormant potential energy force in the human body, that springs up from the root of the spinal cord. In the male body it is believed to be located in the perineum, between the urinary and excretory organs. Whereas, in the female body its location is at the root of the uterus in the cervix. Both these locations within male and female bodies are collectively called the 'muladhar chakra'. This muladhar chakra is in fact a glandular physical structure. The energy force from the kundalini can be awakened through special yogic training and practices of asanas (postures), pranayam (breathing control), kriya (cleansing acts), and meditation (mind control / concentration of mind).

Kundalini yoga is a tantric tradition, wherein the range of mental experience is broadened beyond the framework of time, space and object, and tremendous energy is released within the body. Experiences, which have been subjectively described for thousands of years in the historical past in the names of nirvana, moksha, emancipation, self-realization, salvation, liberation, buddhattva, or Samadhi etc. without understanding them properly are in fact related to only the awakening of kundalini and nothing else. And experiencing physical, mental and psychic state within human body described under such synonymous terminologies like; nirvana, moksha, communion, union, kaivalya, liberation, emancipation, self-realization and salvation, concerning the awakening of kundalini has been the only goal of human spiritual life and of people spending their entire life in pursuit of spirituality [26]. Ignorant man originally named kundalini energy after the Gods, Goddesses, Angles or Divinities and subsequently to the prana shakti. Incidently, the references to the- 'path of the initiates' and the 'stairway to the heavens' as described in the Bible, in fact factually refer to the awakening of the kundalini. The ascent of the kundalini and descent of the experienced spiritual grace that followed from it was symbolized as the Cross, by the Christians. The Cross therefore, symbolically represents the smooth flow of kundalini energy through the power grids called the 'chakras'. The two holes on either side of human spinal cord in cross section are like conduits for all the sensory nerves to pass. These left and right conduits have been given the names as the Ida and pingala nadis respectively. The ida and pingala represent the basic duality, masculine and feminine or the logical and intuitive aspects of life and are called the Shiva and Shakti. Life is created based on this duality. Everything is primordial before duality is created. The terms masculine and feminine do not represent the sex but certain natural qualities in nature, which have been identified to be characteristically masculine and such others as characteristically feminine. Therefore, it is the dominance of the Ida or the pingala that determines the pronounced behavior of any individual, irrespective of donning male or female bodies. ida and pingala have been roughly translated to be respectively controlling the human mind and the body. They (Nadis) do not exist in terms of any physical structures but only in terms of a functional relationship of the prana energy. Vital, life giving prana energy is attributed to the pingala and mind / chitta or consciousness to the ida. Pingala is also defined as the basic, dynamic, active, positive, psychosomatic, masculine, yang energy within human personality responsible for driving the sensory organs. On the contrary, ida is the passive, receptive, negative and feminine yin energy, that controls the sense organs and provides with knowledge and awareness of the world around us [26].

It is our common knowledge that when two equal and opposite forces balance each other, a third force arises. Therefore, when prana energy through ida and pingala are balanced and trigger open the switch at the muladhar chakra, a third force called the sushumna arises. It is only when the sushumna / kundalini is aroused, the prana energy rises sequentially upward from the muladhar to the sahasrasara and provides a blissful experience of realizing union with the universal cosmic consciousness. This is the state according to Carl Jung, of achieving and experiencing a stable, peaceful, divine and dynamically prolonged bliss [26].

A majority of people live and die with their prana energy actively flowing only within ida and pingala nadis. And despite adequate flow of energy prana through ida and pingala and continued effective life possible for an individual, their central space sushumna nadi remains practically dormant. However, sushumna nadi, which is the most significant to human physiology and life really becomes active when prana energy flowing through ida and pingala enters it through the muladhara chakra. The muladhar merely acts as a switch for releasing the flow of kundalini but its actual location rests in the sahasrasara chakra located in brain [26].

The seven chakras namely, the muladhar, swadhisthana, manipur, anahat, vishuddhi, adnya and the sahasrasara, individually exercise control over various organs of the human body and for physically, physiologically, metabolically, mentally and psychologically healthful living. The flow of prana energy through all the seven chakras and three nadis, ida, pingala and sushumna is required to be smooth. In case of any obstruction to its flow at or in between any chakra, the organs under control of that chakra indicate signs of stress or dysfunction and ultimately succumbs to disease or failure with serious consequences, if ignored for long [26].

1.14 Evidence for the existence of nadis, and chakras

The kundalini yoga is based on the premise that there exists a system of thousands and thousands of nadis / conduits spread across the matrix of human body. These nadis distribute the mental, physical and electrical energy through out the body and are intimately linked to the nerves, neurons, blood vessels and to various organs. There is no apparent structural system visible as nadis within human body when dissected. Still however, yogis believe that nadis do exist and their pathways within bodies can be mapped. Nadis are dynamic, live, power conduits for the body and mind. Dr Hiroshi Motoyama[26], a renowned philosopher, psychologist and parapsychologist from Japan is very emphatic about the reality of nadis and the chakras within human body, based on the basis of hundreds of experiments he has conducted. Dr Motoyama[26] has demonstrated a positive correlation between any imbalance, mal-function of nadis and emergence of symptoms of diseases in the body. Intuitively, the author of this book feels very strongly that the ancient concept of nadis is similar, akin or identical to the existence of thousands of ion channels that transmit electrical charges and currents across molecules, cell membranes and in biochemical metabolism within bodis of all conscious organisms as a consequence of the movement and exchange of atomic, electrically charged ions. Discovery of the existence of ion channels is relatively very recent and their importance in understanding of human biology is advancing very rapidly.

Similarly, the painstaking experimental work done by Dr Hiroshi Motoyama [26] and G G Hunt [26] have established a positive correlation with the stimulation of individual chakras by the yoga practitioners and corresponding physiological functional changes in the organs controlled by the respective chakras. Although, no physical or structural demarcation can be located for existence of the chakras within human body, distinct functional characteristics corresponding to the known locations of the seven chakras have been discriminated. The traditional locations of the chakras when activated by the yoga practitioners have also been correlated with corresponding stimulation and vision of characteristic colours, emotions and experiences. All these experiments certainly bring home the fact that the concept of chakras is based on sound para-psycho-phisiological / para-physiological logic and reason. More than this, all phenomena concerning human body and its experiences involving, ida, pingala and sushumna nadis, the kundalini, prana, chakras, soul, mind and consciousness, biochemical metabolic or physical mechanisms, physiology, psychology, emotions, moods, grimaces etc are definitely related to the movement / transfer / sharing of electric charges by means of atomic ions through thousands of ion channels within bodies of conscious organisms.

1.15 What is Death? How does it come about?

Death in a multi-cellular organism is never an instantaneous event, but is known to be a gradual closing down of the process in sequential stages. Brain cells die almost immediately, heart follows next, then kidneys, then the intestines and in the end skin and hair. Eyes retain their usefulness for six hours and must be removed within that period for use in some other individuals [21]. Muscles and nerve cells continue to retain their hold on cells much longer after the individual is dead and therefore stand a chance for a possible revival with immediate electric shock treatment [23] and for use later for a cadaver organ transplant. The fact, that organ transplant is possible, only because the energy that drives these organs is the same in all animal forms and transplanted organs start deriving energy from the ion-channels of the new body in which they are replaced. Avoiding possible rejection of the transplanted organ in a new body is only a matter of re-adjustment of the receptor proteins (memory of its previous body) of the transplanted organ from the cadaver with those of the new body. The Hydrogen protons / electric charges therefore gradually stop flowing through the body as a result of blockage or closure of its essential ion-channels after death. In reality, death only marks the failure of the body system to maintain and regulate the flow of electric charges, mediated through circulation of oxygen in blood vessels and exchange of electric charges through and across cell membranes, neurons, muscles and organs with the help of ions for a continued operation and functions. Maharshi Vashishtha in the Yoga-Vashishtha also mentions- "When on account of the diseases of the body, its Nadis lose their vigour and thus become unable to expand and contract in order to exhale or inhale air, the body loses its harmony and becomes restless. The inhaled air does not properly come out nor does the exhaled air can re-enter the body. So respiration stops and the body, becomes senseless or dead". 'Soul' represents a deeply felt moral and emotional attribute of a universal consciousness with ability to induce or excite and exhibit expressions of kindness, love, affection, gratitude, sympathy, beauty, aesthetics, mood, art, music, anger, rage, hunger and other subtle emotions as consequences of the syntheses and secretion of specific hormones, enzymes, proteins or other metabolites initiated or ignited by particular thought, nature of food consumed, ailment or injury as demanded by the coherent body system under dynamic connection with the universal source of energy / consciousness [23, 43, 46, 47]. This is the reason why it is believed that Souls of all life-forms in the universe share a common inheritance, bond, identity, structure, nature, purpose, work and destiny. No wonder, why we feel tremendous affinity, love, affection, loyalty, concern and complementary purpose for a collective cooperative existence on earth and hold our belief or blind faith in transmigration of Soul between various life-forms possible [43]. Mind borrows its light from the universal electrical potential continuum / cosmic consciousness. Electrons withdrawing or escaping from the various organs to the universe after death, in fact carry memories of the individual organs they were operating for years within the body. And these memories, quite possibly are what

Rupert Sheldrake describes as the 'Morphogenetic memories'. And because, every moment someone or the other is dying on the earth, 'morphogenetic memories' of individual organ parts of the living organisms always remain resonating in the surrounding epigenetic environment from the inherited past, to present and into the future.

Hydrogen (proton/electron) therefore appears to stand appropriate for the identity of the common thread that connects the cosmic energy with the consciousness flowing through all the living organisms. Questionably, if this is possible, it is still a mystery, how hydrogen (proton) or more precisely the magnetic monopoles culminate and get bound into forming a complex composite- a quasi-quantum particulate consciousness called 'Soul' with characteristic attributes and identity of all living organisms?

Much of the confusion has arisen in literature because various specialists indiscriminately use different terminologies for describing essentially the same thing. Thus, energy or frequency pattern mentioned by a physicist, a life-force or information by a biophysicist, GOD by a religious preacher or 'consciousness' and 'soul' by a meta-physicist or a quantum physicist, in fact, synonymously refer to the same common constituent of everything existing in the universe. Therefore, all that has gone into literature on the subject of consciousness needs to be rationalized on standardized with a uniform terminology of common human perceptions in general. Energy, Consciousness / Information or Life force, when slows down, it comes into being 'in-formation' i.e. Coming into form and materialization. Water vapours condensing into liquid and further into solid crystalline ice by cooling exemplify such transformations. Similarly the highly vibrating energy in the universe materializes according to some higher law or principle (still unknown). Plato the Greek Philosopher; suggested that at the most fundamental level, each element is made up of tiny components, each with the shape of a regular solid, assuming only five possible crystalline forms as described by Plato namely, polyhedron, cube, dodecahedron, tetrahedron and octahedron. For this reason, the regular solids are often known as the Platonic solids or Platonic crystals.

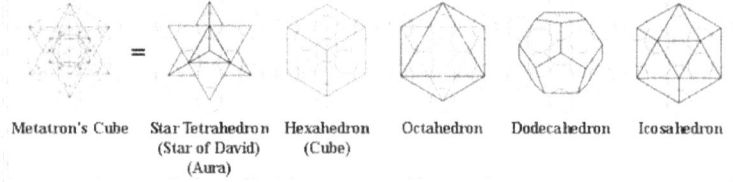

Metatron's Cube (derived from the Fruit of Life) begets the five Platonic solids, including a star tetrahedron (stellated octahedron).

Figure 6. Platonic Crystal Structural Forms

According to Plato's scheme, earth is formed of cubes, fire is formed of tetrahedral, air is formed of octahedral and water is formed of icosahedra. The motivation for this model seems to be the idea that the triangular faces of the tetrahedral, octahedral and icosahedra could be rearranged, like atomic units. This would enable the fundamental tetrahedral, octahedral and icosahedra to transmute into one another, and thereby explain the alchemical transformation of matter from one kind into another. Plato considered the heavens to be eternal and unchanging. Celestial matter, in Plato's view, was therefore composed of a single, perfect fifth element and heavens according to him were associated with the fifth regular solid, the dodecahedron [28].

The geometric form of the crystal formed determines the content of condensed Energy / Life Force / Consciousness / Soul or Information. This condensed energy is stored in the grid-structure of the crystal, called as 'Crystal-Lattice' by the physicists. The term "Cryst-Al" in fact means "All Consciousness". No wonder every kind of matter both animate *(proteins, nucleic acid, cellulose, sugars, carbohydrates)* and inanimate *(salts)* in the universe are crystalline *(Conscious)* in nature as evidenced and elucidated by X-Ray and Electron diffraction techniques. No wonder, 'amorphous materials' beyond limits of detection by X-Ray or Electron diffraction techniques exhibit weird properties.

1.16 Mind as a dynamic responsive attribute and also a reflection of the body interacting with continually changing fluxes of universal energy

The earliest description of the individual 'self' expressed through mind and its identification with the 'universal soul' came from the Vedas and Upanishads which declared– *'aham brahmasmi'* (I am the universal conscious being). The driving force within bodies of conscious organisms and that out in the universe was recognized to be identically same. If this is so, then Hydrogen protons and electrons and their flow as electric currents within nerves, muscles and across cell membranes of bodies of organisms come to mind instantly as they are universally all pervading. **No surprise, neurological symptoms such as loss of consciousness, confusion, forgetfulness, loss of memory, muscular dysfunction, partial or total paralysis of lower limbs, loss of hearing, blindness and sleep disorders are all related and affected by the flow of electric currents.** Dr. Andrew Ure in 1818, demonstrated through his experiments on cadaver body of an extremely muscular man, the sudden revival and commencement of breathing with application of an electric current to the phrenic nerve in the neck [23]. The chest heaved and fell and the belly was protruded and collapsed. The touching of electrode from the battery to the supra-orbital nerve induced the most extraordinary grimaces such as- 'rage, horror, anguish, despair, sober and ghastly smiles' on the face of the cadaver. **Unfortunately, what we do not naturally recognize being the fact that all living organisms are electrical machines and that electric currents lie at the heart of life itself.** But this does not imply that electric charge or current itself is life because electric charges themselves emerge from a still deeper reality in the universe. There is a fundamental difference in the mode between the electricity that powers our bodies and that which lights our cities. Whereas, the electricity supplied to our homes is carried by the negatively charged sub-atomic particles called the electrons, almost all currents in the bodies of living organisms are carried by ions-the electrically charged atoms. Of the five main ions that carry electric currents in our bodies, four are positively charged- sodium+, potassium+, calcium+ and hydrogen+ (protons)- and one, chloride is negatively charged. Movements of electrically charged ions constitute electric currents as nerve impulses that move into and across cell membranes. Electrical impulses travel along the length of our nerve and muscle fibres and the ion currents that generate them flow at right angles to the direction of their travel. Other difference between electric current that lights our homes and the one that power our bodies being in their speeds of transmission. Whereas, an electric signal in a wire travels with the speed of light i.e. 1,86,000 miles per second the electric nerve impulses travel at the speed of mere 0.07 miles per second. The electrical impulses we generate to carry beating of our hearts are only a few millionth of an ampere of current [23]. We have come to understand the origin of bioelectricity and how the molecules (the ion channels) responsible for the electrical activity actually look like since only the last two decades. **Human beings and all other life-forms as part of the nature are being constantly bathed by the terrestrial and universal cosmic energy and our body epigenetically remains in perpetual dynamic interaction with this energy** [47]. **These dynamic interactions are adjustments to the ever fluctuating fluxes of universal energy which create a constantly dynamic demand for secretion or synthesis of proteins, enzymes, co-enzymes or other metabolites in our body systems as a means and matter of survival strategies. The nature of secreted hormones, enzymes, other metabolites together with proteins are responsible for our expressed thoughts, desires, moods and other forms of emotional reactions which are generally characterized and attributed to our enigmatic mind** [39, 43, 47, 48]. No wonder, since the energy fluxes are perpetually changing around us, so also fluctuate our mind, as a part of dynamic adjustment of our body metabolism to the fluctuating universal energy [23, 30, 31, 33, 34, 47]. These are subtle phenomena occurring at quantum or sub-quantum levels. However, we can easily feel, realize, experience and understand them from our reaction, behavior and state of mind when we are exposed to sudden variations in ambient temperature, pressures, climatic and weather conditions and other environmental fluctuations and from the emotional demands generated in our body-mind under those conditions to comfort or ease ourselves [30, 43, 47, 48].

Perhaps modern science will never come to solve the mystery of the soul until and unless the nature and make-up of the most primordial energy from which all other forms of matter are formed is finally resolved. And yet, we find most elaborate and profound descriptions about the constitutional makeup of the soul in the Vedas and Upanishads. These descriptions for over 8,000 years have not been scientifically proved or disproved nor have been surpassed with a more profound concept, theory or thought. No surprise, the Vedic description about the structure and constitution of the 'soul' still continues to rule and tries to satisfy human curiosity. T.D. Singh in presenting, Vedantic model for the interaction of consciousness with matter [48] very rightly suggests that the present scientific research and inquiry should be expanded to include knowledge in search of spiritual truth. What is amazing being that the concepts and ideas about quantized nature of energy and universal existence [39, 49, 50] was factually known to the Saints- 'Rishis' in India almost 8,000 years BC.

1.17 Vedic view of the structure and composition of 'Soul': The 'Panch-Kosh' Siddhanta

It is clear from the discussion given under various sections of this article that a very subtle, highly energetic, quantized form of universal energy is the under-current of all conscious life-forms. This energy is mediated through ion-channels as ionic electric currents within bodies of all life-forms to exhibit their conscious functions. The subtle form of this energy possibly of the kind between pure magnetic (monopoles) and electro-magnetic type, physical laws for its culmination and organization into a complex quantum called the 'soul' for manifestation into conscious life-forms and nature of its quantized behavior are still not known to science, except the knowledge that the whole universe is electrical in nature and behaves as an electric entity [4,21,40,51,52]. But the 'Rishis' and Saints of the Vedic and Upanishadic time in India (8,000 BC) not only pondered over the issue but attempted to describe the structure and constitution of Soul on the basis of 'Panch-Kosh Siddhant' (Five Shell model) an analogue of the modern concept of quantum packets of energy. The five shells of the 'Soul' described in the Veda, namely; 1. Pranamaya Kosha (Concerning Lungs, breathing and beating of the heart. Prana enters the body through the breath and is sent to every cell through circulatory system), 2. Annamaya Kosha (concerning stomach, digestion of food, metabolism and excretion), 3. Dnyanamaya Kosha (concerning mind, sensation and experience), 4. Vidnyanamaya Kosha (concerning knowledge, analysis by brain and perception), and 5. Anandamaya Kosha (concerning the connection and actual source of individual consciousness within body with the universal source) perhaps merely represent the constituent parts of a verigated, multi-organ centric human body, which sustains, operates and functions only because of the electrical current (electric charge) that runs through them. **The Panch-Koshas do not factually represent the structural make-up of the individual 'Soul' but the truth that all functions of respiratory, digestive, excretory and mental systems of all conscious organisms are functionally driven by the 'Electric Energy / Electric Charge' and nothing else.** And for the sake of simplicity and explicit understanding of the human body mechanism, the prana energy / electrical atomic ionic movements has been classified into five kinds depending upon the functions they are used for as; Prana, Apan, Udaan, Saman and Vyan, that control respectively our respiratory, excretory, vocal, olfactory, digestive, muscular and nervous systems. The other ultimate form of the Prana, personified and called as the 'Dhananjaya' remains in the sub-atomic form even after death of the physical body. Intuitively and logically, this should indeed be none other than the electric charge that created, sustained and drove the body as a conscious entity from birth to death and finally escaping back to the universe. This is the only logical scientific explanation that connects well with modern scientific knowledge and the ancient Vedic concept. It is hoped that readers would appreciate, and accept this explanation under the present state of knowledge. Despite classified finer differences based on their functions, the Samaan, Udaan, Vyan, Apaan and Prana energies are essentially same. Prana moves the sense organs or 'Indriyas'. It generates thought, contracts and relaxes muscles, moves body at will, digests food, circulates blood, excretes urine and stool and causes respiration (inhalation and exhalation). It is the Prana that enables us to see, hear, feel, smell, sense, taste and think. The comprehensive and collective origin of all five Pranas is called the 'Hiranyagarbha, the source or the seat of Bramha'. It is the Vyan energy that circulates blood from the heart to all parts of the body through one hundred and one arteries and their seventy two thousand branches.

According to the Taittireeya Upanishad, our physical material body (and that of any living organism) is the 'Annamaiya Kosh' i.e. a shell / packet or body made up of food and juicy fluids. From a length of mere one and half foot at birth, this 'Annamaiya Kosh' elongates to full five or six feet with accumulation of food and juicy fluids with an increasing cell count and weight. Each and every cell of the body has a conscious soul (called the Jeev) in them. The 30 billion individual cells constituting a human body are coherently organized and put to multi-functional (involving integrated work of eyes, nose, ears and those of several organs) work in a cooperative way by the universal consciousness / energy / soul / the 'Prana' or the electric charge. It is this 'Prana' that is believed to stay within 'annamaiya kosh' drives each and every cell and the body as a whole. It dominates, rules and governs all individual jeev-souls of the cells and goads them to synthesize proteins, secrete enzymes, hormones, adenonine tri-phophate (ATP) molecules and other forms of metabolites as demanded by the body, in its continual attempts to dynamically adjust itself to ever changing flux of terrestrial and universal energies as a part of its survival strategy. And these strategies include- laughter, tears, thirst, hunger, rage, anger, love, happiness, satisfaction, physical movement of body, blissfullness and a host of such other emotional states of experiences and responses. The proteins, enzymes, hormones and other biochemicals synthesized within bodies under stimulation by the 'Prana' / universal energy / epigenetic or environmental conditions, generate an important and most enigmatic attribute of the human being called the 'mind' [23, 30, 35, 43, 47]. Since the intensity of the universal conscious energy flux changes every moment, 'mind' which arises as an attribute from dynamic adjustments of body to universal flux of energy also remains continuously flickering. We thus see a deep logical connection and integration of the epigenetic principles with the terrestrial and universal environment in all living organisms as an integral part of nature. 'Mind' as an attribute is also a kind of energy and the location of its generation within mitochondria of each and every cell is also the –'Pranamaiya Kosh'. Since according to modern physics the entire energy in the universe is quantized, mind also must necessarily be quantized. Each and every kind of feeling, emotion, desire, lust, urge etc must be corresponding to differential energy packets of the 'mind quantum' [16, 30, 31, 33-35, 37, 43, 47]. Mind also creates thoughts but to create thoughts, there must be knowledge. Taittireeya Upanishad describes and rests this knowledge as the inner body of the mind and intentionally calls it as the-'Vidnayanmaya kosh' to differentiate it from the universal knowledge- 'Dnyanmayakosh'. There are two categories of consciousness, universal and individual. The Supreme Being (the Prana) is conscious of everything in the universe whereas the living entities (the Jeevas) are conscious of only themselves. The knowledge existing within the 'vidnyanmaya kosh' of mind is only limited and restricted to the appropriate requirement of the biological species to which the body of the living organism (the Jeeva) belongs to [46]. All knowledge about the series of past reincarnations undergone by the living organism remains encoded and stored within this 'vidnyanmaya kosh'. There is always a scope and freedom with the living organism to enlarge, enhance this knowledge and evolve itself into an organism of higher order within a pool of 84,00,000 kinds (Combinations of genes) of possible living species in nature. And to help this evolution, the quantum of universal knowledge called the 'Dnyanmaya kosh' lies always within the very core of the 'vidnyanmaya kosh'. Quantized packets of knowledge, information, learning, memory of incidences, instances, trauma, sufferings of several past rebirths including those of the present birth etc. are encoded and stored within this 'vidnyanmaya kosh' [16, 34, 35, 37, 43]. The last of the quantum body is called the 'anandmaya kosh' wherein resides the primordial, omni-present, omni-potent conscious universal energy, supporting and holding all the outer quantum shells namely; the vidnyanmaya, manomaya, pranamaya and annamaya koshas. The crux of the riddle being, how these, extremely energetic five quantum shells are sequentially connected to each other and what is the nature of the force that binds them together for manifestation and exhibition in the form of a conscious living human organism. Perhaps future developments in quantum chromodynamics (QCD) elucidating strong 'quark-quark' interactions (interactions between the ultimate form of matter) may provide some explanation [50]. The reference to 'sequential connection' mentioned above also suggests the presence of 'Time' ingrained in the manifestation of the 'Panch-Kosh-Soul' as a living organism. And as Halit Eroglu [23] **(pp 49-50)** emphatically suggests and innovatively interprets- "When defining the time as the period between two events, then the time, or more specifically, a certain timing cycle, is the actual cause of the events. Without time, physical processes cannot take place, because there would be no "pulse" which could be addressed by the events. The events in the smallest dimensions do not take place themselves, while time is running alongside, but it is the quantized timing cycle which causes the events with its periodic sequences. All physical processes (therefore) depend on a universal timing cycle, whose sum we measure as an ordinary time, as Time Arrow, upon which the Cause-Effect principle is based. The time occurs in the smallest dimension and develops into bigger dimensions through the summation. Therefore our time interval of a 'second' on a macroscopic scale is the sum of the quantized timing cycles in the Planck dimension. In the Planck sphere, there is plenty of time for the quantum events. The measured time is therefore dependent on the size of the scale. While on earth millions of years pass according to our time measurement, for an observer in the quantity of several million light years only some seconds would have elapsed according to his clock".

Quite recently, Amit Goswami [50] in his brilliant book has attempted to describe the relationship between quantum physics and consciousness in describing the constitution of Soul which he calls as a 'Quantum monad' and readers are recommended to refer to this for comprehensive details.

In the end, I would just like to say that I have not discovered the Soul. There is no such claim from my side for there had never been a thing like Soul in nature. For thousands of years, it has just been our chase for the proverbial- wild goose called the Soul. Electrical charge is the fundamental reality and it is electric charge that forms, sustains and disintegrates material structures and drives the universe from stars, planets, galaxies to inanimate and animate matter. Electric charge is the *de facto* Soul, and it is this mighty force that recycles everything in this universe. Electron does not decay like other particles and has a life span of **10^{66}** years. Everything described in respect of the Soul for thousands of years and all attributes assigned to it are equally true and scientifically applicable to electron and their behavior (electric charge).

CHAPTER 2

Questions about Soul and Rebirth: Need for a fresh look and re-definition

2.1 Abstract

The concepts of Soul and Re-birth have been connected with human life and psyche ever since the Vedic civilization (20,000 BC). Practically every religion and every civilization on the earth, irrespective of geographical location, nationality, levels of educational, scientific and technological developments have believed in existence of soul and concept of rebirth. However, tremendous developments in science (particularly physics and biology) and increase in level of instrumental detection and resolution limits since the beginning of the 20 th century, have not only changed human life but have revolutionized our thoughts, concepts, perceptions and views about the whole gamete of energy, matter, space, time, consciousness and nature of reality in the universe. All these developments, call for an entirely new approach to looking at all our traditional concepts and their interpretations, purely on the basis of science and scientific logic, developed since the beginning of the 20th century. It has been argued that the activities of a conscious organism, generally attributed to the 'Soul' are nothing but the result of the electric charges and flow of electrically charged atomic ions and ionic currents across bio-molecules and cellular membranes through millions of ion channels established within developing and developed bodies of both uni- and multi-cellular, multi-organ living entities. Similarly, it has been logically argued that there is no possibility of any individual taking a re-birth after death. The whole concept of re-birth is linked to the memory of an individual previously born and lived in the past and perpetuated in the minds of individuals or in social memory through historical records. In the absence of such memory or record, the concept of re-birth of an individual from a historical past loses all its meaning, relevance and significance. Developments in modern physics, suggest no such possibility for a re-birth of an individual after death from the past. However, it provides ample scope, opportunities and provision for the culmination of conditions, irrespective of time frames, locations, parentage, religious beliefs, nationalities, colour of skin and sex of an individual, to be born with characteristics, properties and traits of head, heart and valour, similar or near exactly similar in resemblance to one who had been born earlier in the historical past. And memories about whom have been preserved in social memory and documented records. In this context, it has been argued, that stories about Shrikrishna and Gautam Buddha remembering all of their past births and re-births cannot be factually true. These stories about Shrikrishna and Buddha remembering their births and re-births have descended to us from third person accounts. And there is likely possibility of a distortion or mis-interpretation percolating down for centuries without rethinking, introspection, reasoning or questioning. Therefore, these stories merely appear to be the metaphoric personal examples cited on behalf of Shrikrishna and Gautam Buddha for explaining the factual reality and law of perpetual creation, temporary subsistence and destruction of all material (both inanimate and animate inclusive) going on in the universe and nothing more. It has therefore been pleaded that, when developments in science and technology are driving the twenty first century, scientists must come forward to explain and re-interpret our traditional concepts, purely on the basis of modern science, developed particularly after the beginning of 20th century, without any fear and free from personal, social, religious biases and dogmatic belief. It is now known that the entire universe constitutes nothing but an inter-play of matter and energies of various kinds governed only by four kinds of natural forces namely; weak and strong interactions, electromagnetic and gravitation. And all material in the universe is made of Atoms and structures built from them. All Atoms in the universe are available in only 118 different kinds and that too in very limited proportions and quantities. These

'Atoms' themselves are 'Conscious entities' simply because of the fact that, they all have retained their individual nature, properties and characteristics besides their personal identities as to 'Who they are', ever since they were first created in the nuclear furnaces of stars during the 'Big-Bang' explosion, that occurred about 14 billion years ago. The author believes that modern developments in the fields of Molecular biology, Epigenetic, Biocentrism, Chemical Kinetics, Morphogenetic Fields, Stellar Chemistry, String Theory and Standard Model of particle physics can be used in a multi-disciplinary way to explain our traditional concepts on modern scientific logic. We cannot afford to leave our twenty first century generation to remain scientifically unaware, ignorant and continue to remain as victims of out-dated religious dogmatic belief, ignorance and blind faith and continue to oppose new science. The author is hopeful that the readers would sincerely introspect and appreciate his frustration and dilemma in comprehending and understanding the traditional concepts as are being described in innumerable books in a traditional way.

Questions about Soul and Rebirth: Need for a fresh look and re-definition

2.2 Introduction

Ever since the beginning of the most ancient Vedic civilization and Vedic philosophy that flourished in India almost 20,000 years BC [1-3], the concept of 'Soul' has remained attached to the human life, psyche and thought. This concept has also been upheld by other religious philosophies and civilizations that have followed and flourished on earth irrespective of geographic locations, nationalities, scientific and technological developments, colour of inhabitants and levels of education. The singular oldest 'Vedic concept of Soul' must have, probably and logically, spread globally by word of mouth through frequent travelers, merchants and scholars who came to India from different lands and returned back to their natives or by those preachers from India who either voluntarily travelled on their own or were sent by the feudal Kings to different lands for the purpose of spreading the message of Vedas and Upanishads. Vedas are the oldest known philosophical texts in the world that form the tenets of the Sanatan Hindu Way of living [4]. Later in history, Emperor Ashok, is reported to have deliberately sent teams of scholars and preachers to distant and neighboring lands to spread Buddhist philosophy and ideology. No wonder, places connected to Buddha are still found from Afghanistan in the West of India to China in North, to Myanmar (Burma) and Japan in the East and to the South-East in Sri-Lanka (Ceylon), Malaysia (Malaya), Thailand, Combodia and Indonesia. In view of the missing links and documentary record on visits and travels of each and every one of those who came to the Indian sub-continent, there is merit, logic and also reason to believe that the 'concept of soul' in varying forms, shades, definitions and ideas might have also independently originated, evolved or refined by civilizations in other places. Whatever may be the truth, the concept of 'Soul' has factually remained as one of the most profound enigmatic mysteries to human beings until today. No surprise, the 'Soul' and its integration with religions, mind and spirituality should have virtually driven 'crazy', millions of men and women from all parts of the world to search for it, discover it, feel or sense it, visualize, understand, realize, identify, explain and even describe it as a common thread that binds all conscious living creatures together on Earth and possibly in the universe. Today, all civilizations, religious groups, philosophies in the world accept and regard the 'Soul' as something that drives the entire animate kingdom from humans, animals, insects, fish and plants to the unicellular organisms. Although some evidence has been claimed about soul taking a rebirth and life after-death [5-9] there is no unanimity over the concept and belief on rebirth of 'Souls' and their transmigration between and across species of all life forms for various reasons. The 'Soul' as a common constituent of all living entities is considered and believed to be universal and indestructible. Surprisingly, where is then the question of its birth, death and rebirth? The conscious mobility of living entities supposedly done at the instance of the 'Soul' is in fact the attribute and handy work of electric charge and ionic currents [10] depending upon the nature and kind of atoms involved which themselves are conscious entities [11]. The bodies of living creatures constitute nothing more than a lump of ordinary matter comprising of atoms of predominantly few specific kinds and 'Mind' appears to be an attribute arising out of the collective experience, feelings and electrical activity of thousands of kinds of bio-molecular proteins, synthesized within millions of individual cells of the body as a part of its coherent strategy for survival, in response to the continually changing environment [10, 12]. Therefore, each and every cell of the body, according to Candace B. Pert [12] constitutes the 'Mind'. Mind is regarded as the owner of experiences and feelings, the center or focus of thoughts. And according to David Hume ('A Treatise of Human Nature' ed. P H Nidditch; Oxford University Press, 1978; first published 1739, Book-I, Part-IV, Chapter 6)- " the self is nothing but a collection of experiences: When I enter most intimately into what I call myself, I always stumble upon some particular perception or other, of heat or cold, light or shade, love or hatred, pain or pleasure. I can never catch myself at any time without a perception, and never can observe anything but only perception".

2.3 A case of factual reality and redefining rebirth

Extraordinary human individuals are immortalized by society in public memory because of their morals, thoughts, literary contribution, work, ideals, actions, valour and compassion they stand for, than for the size of their physical body, appearance and physique. Thousands of years after Shrikrishna mentioned about remembering his own, innumerable births and re-births in the Geeta, it was Gautam Buddha who has been reported to have distinctly remembered all his past births and deaths which include **357** lives as a human beings, **66** as Gods and **123** as animals, indicating thereby a suggestive possibility of trans-migration from human to 'godly angelic' individuals to the animal life forms in between successive births. Surprisingly however, there is neither mention nor description of the sequential order of the births and rebirths of Gautam Buddha. In both these cases, it is impossible to believe that both Shrikrishna and Gautam Buddha should have factually remembered their individual identity all through the cycles of their births, deaths and rebirths. It seems more probable, reasonable, logical and scientifically consistent to believe that both Shrikrishna and Gautam Buddha, being knowledgeable about Vedic philosophy and Upanishads, were in fact, citing their own lives, deaths and re-births as metaphoric examples in explaining the cardinal principle of perpetually cyclic nature of material creation, existence and destruction going on in the universe. And this cycle is common to both the inanimate and animate matter and nothing more. It is perhaps our enamoured love, affection, appreciation and emotional attachment to the personalities, qualities and teachings of both Shrikrishna and Gautam Buddha individually, that have blinded us to overlook the factual scientific truth in their statements and mistakenly assume them to being endowed with super-natural powers. Both, Shrikrishna and Gautam Buddha were human beings like any other individual. Shrikrishna was bestowed and invoked with God-hood more than 2500 years after his death as per records mentioned by Dr. P. V. Vartak [13], and Gautam Buddha, during his own life time, had clearly emphasized that he was neither a GOD nor a messenger of a GOD. His enlightenment was not the result of a supernatural prowess, power, process or agency, but rather the result of close and minute attention he paid to the nature of the human mind which could be rediscovered by anyone for himself.

2.4 Possible role of synthesized proteins in controlling behavior, actions and in state of enlightenment

Enlightenment is a process of being developed. It represents an emotional state of complete transformation from within and sprouts from the inner depth of a focused mind with full force of concentrated urge [14.] And obviously, this type of complete transformation can only be possible by controlling the induced synthesis of the kind and nature of specific hormones, proteins and glandular secretions by controlling thoughts and concentrating Mind. It is well known that emotions and experiences are strongly influenced by physical effects, such as sound and the chemical composition of the blood and hormonal imbalances. No wonder, why Vedas, Upanishads and the Geeta, emphasize on controlling thoughts by way of practicing meditation [2, 3, 12, 14]. It is now scientifically known for sure that our thoughts control the secretion of hormones and synthesis of proteins in the body, proteins control and modify metabolic, muscular and physiological behavior that ultimately leads to physical actions and their reactions [12]. Our five senses, together, form a single integrated sensory system that is essentially designed to perceive a physical reality and man creates his own reality through action and thoughts [15]. Therefore, enlightenment essentially means to learn to control thoughts, concentrate and focus mind to control secretion of hormones to control the synthesis, nature, kind and extent of specific proteins as a consequence. The state of mental and body condition, experienced under the influence of such specifically induced and synthesized proteins by way of meditative practices, may possibly be the experienced blissful state, to what we call 'the enlightenment'. The very fact, that a rigorous practical training in controlling mind for years, according to eight principles of performing yoga i.e. Yama, Niyama, Asana, Pranayam, Pratyahara, Dharana, Dhyana and Samadhi as described by Patanjali, is essentially required to be able to experience such a blissful condition, probably indicates the factual truth of this phenomena and reality and its linkage to proteins. Whereas, Yama, Niyama and Asana form the principle at the physical level, the Pranayam and Pratyahara operate at the level of the mind and essentially concern with exercises in breathing for regulation of mind and energy and controlling the deviation of mind to the external world through five senses. Truly speaking the vocabulary for explaining the exact stage / state of what we call 'enlightenment' has not yet been born [15] but the role of synthesized proteins under strict control of mind in meditation, seems most logical scientific possibility. The other attributes induced and expressed by the human beings, as a consequence of the syntheses and secretion of specific hormones, enzymes, proteins or other metabolites within body, initiated or ignited by particular thoughts, food consumed, ailment, injury, inhalation or excitement etc. being, the expressions of kindness, love, affection, gratitude, sympathy, beauty, aesthetics, mood, art, music, anger, rage, hunger, sex, allergies and such other subtle emotions.

2.5 Religious philosophies are based on third-person accounts

It is a historical fact that stories about the life, work and philosophy of both Shrikrishna and Gautam Buddha and also in respect of Jesus Christ, Prophet Mohammad and Lord Mahavir were written, compiled or interpreted by their followers long after they were gone. Neither of them had told nor even written their own biographies. Information about all of them has descended down to us from the records written by third persons, either contemporary or otherwise. The 'Mahabharata' itself has seen three editions before coming into the present form from originally containing 8,800 verses written by Ved Vyasa to 24,000 verses in the version edited by Rishi Vaishampayan and finally to 100,000 verses in the version compiled and edited by Rishi Sauti, sequentially within a span of about one thousand years from Ved Vyas **('The Three Editions of the Mahabharata' by N.R. Waradpande, Free download from Website: www.nrwaradpande.in).** Moreover, according to Swami Shivananda, there is practically no reference to rebirth in the early part of the Vedic literature and no stigma of sin or dreaded life of the hell-fire and no heavenly lure for the mortals. But as the Vedic mind progressed from polytheistic concept to the monistic ideals of the one, absolute reality at the beginning of the 'Aranyaka period', the doctrine of soul was evolved as a logical necessity in order to safeguard an unsullied existence of GOD in human thought and mind. Therefore, there appears to be something fundamentally wrong or quite possibly a distortion in communication and in understanding the messages of both, Shrikrishna and Gautam Buddha about the factual reality or mystery of remembering their own births and rebirths. Even in the case of Shri Ram in the epic 'Ramayana', he has been essentially described as an ordinary human being all through the text, except a brief mention to his (Ram's) being an incarnation in the 'Bal-Kaand' and 'Sunder-Kaand' chapters.

Innumerable instances have, again been documented, at least in case of the well known enlightened Saints, Prophets, Rishis and Spiritually pious people, wherein they temporarily appeared in physical forms, simultaneously at different locations to help or guide their disciple or relation in difficulty. If such appearances are factually true, then why these should not be considered as the cases of simultaneous rebirths of the same individual, because he or she is carrying all his personal traits and qualities with himself / herself to be justified as a rebirth? Forget for the time being, the mode of such appearances or how this is possibly done and explainable on the basis of quantum physics. In comparison to this argument it is clear, why identical twins or identically looking 'father-son' or 'mother–daughter' combinations cannot be considered as rebirths or simultaneous rebirths because such individuals are entirely different in their personal characteristics, except in physical looks. 'Rebirth' in that event, needs to be re-defined and need not be considered to be restricted to being born only after death in previous life in a sequential order, irrespective of the irregular time gap between successive deaths and rebirths. Without consideration of the concept of 'free will', all natural processes are bound to be regularly cyclic and periodic. Incidentally, all stories about rebirths, therefore, appear to have possibly survived and prevailed for thousands of years under the dogmatic influence of religious thoughts and continued belief in the existence of something unknown and called the 'Soul' or 'Super-intelligence', at the back of our mind and grooming since childhood. No wonder, almost all scientific books, published until the end of the 19th century, invoked the element of GOD and his divine hand in one way or the other. Even the most revolutionary scientist of all times, Sir Isaac Newton was not free from the dogmatic bondage with religious yoke. Tremendous developments in science and technology starting from the beginning of the 20th Century, have completely revolutionized our perceptions and concepts about the nature, forms, manifestations and interactions of energies, universe, material creation and reality. Subjects such as; Soul, Mind, Consciousness, Mind-Matter interactions, Telepathy, Tele-transportation, Clairvoyance, spirituality etc. which have dominated human life and psyche for thousands of years are no longer considered to be un-scientific and exclusive domains of religion, religious preachers and philosophies. They need to be integrated with physical sciences as part and parcel of the continual inter play of universal energy-matter continuum and laws that govern their interactions. Soul, consciousness, mind, psyche and such entities, in whatever form and kind of energy they might be manifesting, cannot be different but must form a part and parcel of our universal creation. No wonder these subjects today are being profusely funded by government and private funding agencies for putting them on rational modern scientific logic and foundation. Acharya Rajneesh (Osho) was perhaps right when he said– "Religions that do not evolve themselves in line with modern science and technology, will have no option but to die". It is therefore imperative on the part of global scientific community to look dispassionately to these subjects and to the traditionally inherited concepts for thousands of years from purely scientific point of view and justifiably interpret them more as problems of multi- and inter-disciplinary continuum of modern scientific knowledge, developed only after the beginning of the 20th Century. If the Religious leaders do not volunteer and take initiative to integrate religion with modern science, the scientific community must take such initiative in explaining the illusive religious /metaphysical concepts on scientific theories. It cannot be denied that science also has something to say about religious matters. Topics such as the nature of time and space, the origin and nature of matter and life, or causality, free-will and determinism etc. the very conceptual framework in which the religious questions have been posed can be altered by scientific advances. Some of the theological issues of centuries past have been rendered meaningless by modern cosmology and science. Even Albert Einstein admitted that- "We believe that science serves humanity best when it is all free of influence by any dogma and reserves the right to question all assumptions, including their own" and "It is more difficult to break a prejudice than an atom".

2.6 Our criteria for considering and accepting re-birth

The only justified measure / criteria so far, for our consideration for belief in accepting rebirth has been the accidental birth of an individual, born in an entirely different time scale and location, under entirely different combination of genetic, epigenetic, environmental, terrestrial and celestial configurations, conditions and circumstances, matching exactly or near-exactly in similarities and characteristics of personality, traits and quality of certain exalted thoughts, ideals, sagacity, behavior, action and leadership with any person, who had been born earlier in the historical past and memories about whom are perpetually ingrained in our social memory or in documentary records. In the absence of such a memory or documented history, the question of rebirth loses all significance and relevance. The physical body, appearance, characteristics, parentage, geographic location, nationality, religious faiths or year and time of birth, practically are given no consideration except exact or near exact correspondence of qualities of head, heart and thoughts in deciding a rebirth of an individual from the past. It is again a practical social truth that any individual born with corresponding characteristics of personalities and brilliance of Shrikrishna or Gautam Buddha even today, will cast his influence and spell over the society around him and reform it. The Uncertainty Principle, enunciated by Werner Heisenberg, states that no two events are exactly alike and statistical probability for such incidences to coincide may be one in billions. That leaves no scope for a possible rebirth of an individual from the past after his death but at the same time suggests considerable possibility for an individual to be born in future with characteristic traits of quality of head, heart and mind similar or nearly similar to anyone who had previously lived on the earth, because the entire universe contributes to what we are. Perhaps, the meaning of the well cited and very often repeated couplet from the Geeta –" Yada yada hee dharmasya, glaneerbhavati Bharat, Abhyuthanamdharmsya tadatmaanum srujamyaham; Paritranaya sadhunam, vinashaya cha dushkrutam, Dharmasansthapanarthay, Sambhavaamee yugey yugey"(O Bharata, whenever there is decay of dharma (foundation required for the healthy progress of life), leading to chaos (rise of adharma), I embody Myself (to halt deterioration and put evolution on proper track). For the protection of the righteous and the destruction of the wicked, as well as for the strengthening of the foundation of dharma, I am born time and again. **(Geeta Chapter 4, Verses 7, 8, Ref 14, pp 112-113)** essentially conveys this scientific message and nothing more [16].

The belief in rebirth is attempted to be justified by advancing an argument that the living 'Soul' of the creature carries memory of its actions, learning and characteristic attributes to its new birth after death. There is no unanimity over how exactly this is possible, and on the nature and structure of the 'Soul' for this to be true, on the nature of forces or energies that are involved in transfer of memory from Soul in one life to that in the other? This justification, instead of satisfactorily answering the problem has raised new questions on the exact location of memory in the body; how, where and what organ is involved; in what form they are recorded, stored and recalled; nature and form of the vehicle and mode of transferring memory during cycles of birth-death and rebirths. Here, even if we assume for the time being, that the Soul itself carries his memories from one life to the other as the vehicle of transfer, the 'Garbha-Upanishad', on the contrary clearly states that a fetus growing in the womb of its mother itself becomes Jeeva (conscious self) in the seventh month and becomes complete in every sense to be a person in the eighth month. Clearly, in the seventh month of growing stage of fetus, the developing ion channels in its body become fully operational to exchange ions and conduct ionic currents i.e. it is the stage at which the ionic electric currents begin flowing and consciousness (as electrical activity) appearing or analogically the soul entering the fetal body. The fully developed fetus as a person by the end of the eighth month is believed to forget all memories of its past lives, births, deaths and acts before birth [17]. Here again, there is an unjustified assumption that the fetus had carried its memories from the past until then, when it, itself comes to the conscious state in the eighth month. The 'Sarvasa Upanishad' however mentions that a 'subtle body (Linga Deha) is created as an attribute out of the mind and other subtle elements that reside in the knot of the heart and the consciousness within this body is the 'knower of the field'. What is this subtle element that resides in the knot of the heart? Has it got something to do with the power grid of consciousness called the- 'Anahata Chakra or the 'Heart Chakra' which creates the field of coherence around the body? Obviously, answers to these questions are not easy, but in attempts to justify and support the devised line of thinking, theories on trans-migration of memory from one life to the other were also invented, developed and invoked. The theory of 'Karma' from the Vedic times to the theory of 'Morpho-Genetic Fields' and 'Morphic-Resonance' by Rupert Sheldrake [18, 19-22] in recent years are the most popular examples. Still however, both these theories representing bold attempts for explaining rebirth and mode of transfer of memory from one life to other, fundamentally pre-suppose the existence of Soul to be a factual reality of animate and inanimate material creation in nature. Perhaps, the memory of our dogmatic socio-religious thought, perpetuated in our personal, community and social life system for thousands of years, about the existence of some super-intelligence, at the back of our thinking is preventing us from taking an objective fresh look, purely from the scientific point of view.

2.7 Everything in the Universe is Made of Atoms

It is now known that, our physical existence is nothing more than an ordinary part of the cyclic creation of animate and inanimate matter in nature, under control of only four kinds of natural forces, namely the weak and strong interactions, electromagnetic and gravitation. Everything in the animate and inanimate material world is made of atoms and it is the kind, nature, proportions, conditions, environment and configuration of their combinations together that determine the physical form, chemical properties, characteristic traits and behavior of all kinds of the structures formed. During the 20th Century, we have learned that living and lifeless matter do not differ in any fundamental way. There is no definite stage of complexity at which life appears, and there is no definite stage of evolution at which minds develop in living organisms. Therefore, consciousness and memory appear to be ingrained in the atoms and their structures themselves. The 118 different kinds of atoms available in whatever limited quantities, in nature today, were created at the time the 'Big-Bang' occurred. All these atoms have retained their identities (and of course the memory of who they are) ever since then. It is pertinent to ask, if our own memory is a culmination of the combined probability attribute of the individual memories of all atoms that constitute our body; or that of the 'Soul' if it factually exists; or more particularly that of the varying nature, kind and amount of thousands of proteins synthesized within our body system? Perhaps the last possibility, appears to be scientifically more realistic than others because proteins in living organisms, have a flexible structure, very little thermal disorder at room temperatures and despite not being liquids, they move freely and exhibit the properties of consciousness [11]. Our soul has also been logically and analytically described to be an attribute of ionic currents and electrical activity of all the atoms that constitute our bodies [10, 23] and it is likely that we have failed to recognize electric charge (hydrogen proton and electron, its negative equivalent to be the *de-facto* 'Soul' that drive all conscious creatures [10]. And if this is so, then why an individual, ridden with Alzheimer's disease should lose his memory and identity can possibly be explained on the basis of the nature, kind and amounts of new proteins synthesized in his body [12] after contracting the ailment. As, we know, we cannot predict when a man will die, but we can certainly predict how many men from each category of individual age groups will die in a year, in a country or from a community, on the basis of modern quantum physical methods.

Joel Steinheimer, a renowned quantum physicist and mathematician, in his remarkable studies on epigenetic regulation of biosynthesis of proteins in plants, translates especially composed, audible musical vibrations into corresponding quantum vibrations that occur at the molecular level as a protein is being assembled in a plant from its constituent amino acids. By using simple physics, Steinheimer [24] composes musical notes that achieve this correlation. Each musical note which he composes for the plant is a multiple of original quantum frequencies that occur when the quantum-particulate molecules of amino acids join to assemble the protein chain. Playing the right kind of musical tune stimulates the formation of a plant's protein and increases its growth. The length of a note corresponds to the real time it takes for each amino acid to join next during the assembly of protein molecular structure [24]. Steinheimer's research [24] clearly brings out that the characteristics and experiences of a plant are determined by the external epigenetic environment and by the nature and kind of induced synthesized proteins by the stimulus from external (and also internal) environment during growth.

2.8 Need for a new thinking and explanation on our traditional concepts

Even in case we assume that some form of soul persists beyond death, it remains to be explained what particles of material or non-material stuff is that soul made of? What kind and nature of known or unknown forces hold it to the animate life forms and how does it interact with ordinary matter? Unfortunately, nobody from the advocates of the existence of souls, their trans-migration and life-after-death, has tried to sit down and do the hard work of explaining how the basic physics of atoms that constitute the entire universal animate and inanimate material creations, consisting of electrons, protons and neutrons beyond rules laid down by the 'Standard Model of Particle Physics and Quantum Physics' would have to be altered, used or interpreted in order for this to be true. Humanity has so far remained divided on this account for various reasons which have been effectively summarized by Moharir [10] in his comprehensive multidisciplinary review on the subject. Stories about rebirth of souls and their transmigration are enjoying credence and circulation in all languages, communities, societies and nationalities irrespective of nature and form of political systems and levels of scientific and technological developments. Moharir [10] in this holistic article has attempted to describe the concept about 'Soul' on the basis of modern scientific logic, and has pleaded for evolving a universal consensus opinion for rationalization and standardization of various terminologies, free from socio-religious fears, personal biases, prejudices, preferences and dogmas, being indiscriminately used by people from different disciplines in essentially describing the same thing. As a consequence, the energy or frequency pattern mentioned by a physicist, a life-force or information by a biophysicist, GOD by a religious preacher or 'consciousness' and 'soul' by a meta-physicist or a quantum physicist, in fact, synonymously refer to the same common constituent of everything existing in the universe. The confusion prevalent with regards to inconsistent conflicting ideas and concepts in this area of research needs to be removed. Literature, on the subject of 'Soul' written with limited narrow traditionally philosophical, psychological, religious, cultural, emotional and dogmatically personal biases have complicated and confused the situation more than resolved for greater clarity despite tremendous advancements in science, technology and limits of instrumental resolution. Rarely has anyone described (or at least attempted to describe) the subject of 'Soul' from a holistic multidisciplinary perspective. No wonder, our understanding about 'Soul' and 'Mind' continue to be mysteriously enigmatic, confusing and dogmatically bound to the traditional yoke. It is high time to at least attempt to resolve the matter for good and set all speculations, fallacies, fictions and subjective imaginations to rest, purely and almost exclusively on the strength of scientific logic and truth. This is particularly important in view of the fact that research on subjects like, soul, mind, consciousness, mind-matter interactions, clairvoyance, spirits and spirit-world etc. are receiving increasing research funding on global scale. Moreover, in the twenty first century, when developments in scientific and technological areas are driving the civilization, we cannot allow humanity to remain a continued victim of ignorance, illiteracy, superstitions, blind faith, confusion and continue to bear the burden of dogmatic religious views any more. It is the moral duty and responsibility of the Global scientific community and scientific academies in particular to rise above narrow considerations of dogmas of various shades of opinions and educate the common man on the basis of scientific facts. Therefore, all that has gone into literature on the subject of Soul needs to be rationalized on standardized uniform terminology of common human perceptions in general. There is therefore no reason, excuse or justification on the part of any of our religious leaders to remain themselves, irresponsibly ignorant, aloof, isolated or blind-folded from the developments in modern science and to keep their followers scientifically unaware, ignorant, illiterates and brain-washed to remain dogmatically opposed to new scientific thinking. They first need to open-up themselves, develop capacity to understand the new science, evolve with changing time, accept reality and help in providing a scientific basis to their faiths before preaching to newer generations because, the only purpose of religions is to collectively and individually educate their followers to live mentally, thoughtfully, intellectually, knowledgably, academically, physiologically, nutritionally and physically in sound good health in harmony with the laws of nature. **It is therefore heartening, in contrast to the known history and traditionally orthodox and dogmatic attitude of the Vatican Church, that Pope Francis has recently in 2014 AD, should have voluntarily endorsed the Scientific theories of 'Evolution' and 'Big Bang' to be factual realities. How I wish, the Islamic Religious leaders from all nationalities also take a cue in this direction and help their followers in liberating themselves from out-dated dogmatic yokes.**

Keeping in correspondence with the developments in modern science and technology, the ancient 'Vedic' and 'Upanishad' philosophies (20,000 BC) from India, surprisingly, stand tall and scientifically relevant to a large extent even today. But unfortunately, the scholars here are not even educating and explaining the fundamental science described in the Vedas, Upanishads and Geeta to the common men. They continue to merely keep repeating and telling stories and performing the ritualistic practices, traditions and superstitions without reason, question or independent rethinking. No surprise, the perfectly scientific treatises, such as 'Vedas' and 'Upanishads' should continue to be erroneously described under 'Hindu Religious literature'. Unfortunately, Sanskrit language scholars from India rarely understand modern science and Scientist (Physicists) on their part neither learn nor understand Sanskrit. No wonder, why, ignorance, misconceptions, misunderstanding, confusion and even incorrect interpretations of Vedic teachings continue to prevail amongst larger section of masses. The author without any reservation, heed of what others might think of him, has no hesitation in admitting that with all intellectual honesty, his own attempts to sincerely understand the concepts of soul, consciousness, mind and re-birth etc. literally made his head hurt. Even, reading the best of available scholarly books written by celebrated authorities, from various segments of religious and philosophical schools, without bias, malice, prejudice, doubts or intentions of questioning their sincerity, honesty, convictions and authority in attempting to write their own thoughts through these books, have personally not been able to provide him (author) clear mental images, or comprehension about these concepts. Perhaps, the author himself lacks the kind of necessary sophistication to fully conceive all that is described in these books, when millions of other readers have rocked their heads, tamely accepted and surrendered to their contents. They all have appeared to him (to the author), a myriad collection of beautifully worded, strongly motivating, emotionally charged, masterly skilled, psychologically captivating and mentally paralyzing and yet, profound literary compositions of choicest words and phrases, subjectively presenting individual perceptions but still demanding clarity on the basis of modern scientific theories. **The present article is therefore an outcome and reflection of the frustration suffered by the author in seeking to understand these concepts, which have been boggling human mind since time immemorial. I hope, my readers would appreciate my sincere urge, hopeless frustration, dilemma in my pursuit and convictions. Perhaps they may patiently introspect, and possibly indentify themselves with me and justify the arguments raised in this article. They may even find themselves in no better situation than me. Optimistically, a ray of hope may be seen in someone from somewhere on the horizon provoked from such an introspection.**

The author is also of sincere convictions that a holistic plausible explanation for Soul, consciousness, mind, memory and rebirth can be sought within the framework of multi- and inter-disciplinary approach involving tenets of new theories on epi-genetics, biocentrism, morphogenesis, morphic resonance, chemical reaction kinetics, stellar chemistry, quantum physics, quantum chromo-dynamics, String Theory, the Standard Model of Atomic Structure and molecular biology [25-33]. We have perhaps not listened carefully to what Nature has been trying to convey through the modern developments in physics, without some kind of dogmatic bias at the back of our minds that all matter (Atoms) has a rudimentary degree of consciousness and that man and all animate life forms are a direct result of this property of matter OR that of various kinds of field-attributes generated by the matter under specific constitution and configurations. Quantum mechanics, to that extent is a mathematical description of the consciousness of matter [11].

Dr Vidyadhar Gopal Oke, a renowned medical specialist and an innovative musicologist has recently published his book on rebirth / reincarnation in Marathi ("Poonarjanma- Mithya Kee Tahtya" Param Mitra Publications, Thane, Maharashtra, 2018, pp 259). The author has collected and published data on personal attributes, characteristics, qualities, facial similarities and level of excellence achieved in the field of music on a large number of individuals from both within and outside India, who had lived in the historical past and compared them with those who are either currently living today or were living until very recently. Based on such purely arbitrary comparison and similarities, the author has called such correspondence of characteristics and attributes as plausible rebirth of those who had lived in the historical past in the person of those who are living today. And in doing so, the author has not probed, explored, investigated and considered any genetic or family inheritance, linkages, connection or relation etc. in arriving at his conclusions about plausible rebirth / reincarnation of the individuals from the historical past. We believe or tend to believe in the concept of 'rebirth' or 'reincarnation' because we are aware, knowledgeable and conscious about the exemplary characteristics of individuals who had lived in the past from documentary records or public memory. In the absence of such documentary records or vocal transfer of memories from one generation to the other, perhaps the very concept of a 'rebirth' or 'reincarnation' may not have been born. Therefore, the very concept of 'rebirth' appears to have been incorrectly interpreted, understood and conceptualized all through the history of thousands of years of our generations in the past. There is certainly a 'rebirth or reincarnation' in nature, but it is only that of the 'Self-Replicating DNA molecules' and definitely not of any individual human being after his or her death. DNA is the only self replicating molecules in nature for millions of years of our evolutionary history. It is the DNA which keeps on generating individuals with a certain set of relatively good or bad characteristics or excellence in any kind of trade, practices, knowledge or professional aptitude as a part of the routine cycle of its self-replicating process. In this respect, every individual human being is potentially born as a Krishna or Buddha or Jesus and their characteristics are perennially ingrained and present in his or her DNA. It is only the epigenetic conditions (inclusive of cosmological, terrestrial, physical, physiological) during conception, development and growth in the uterus of mother, nutrition availability, food intake by the mother and her mental status etc. are primarily responsible for the expression of only certain combination of genes in response to such epigenetic conditions to determine the personality of the child born. In this process, only few genes are reported to be functional whereas 90% of the genes (junk DNA) are believed to remain inactive despite their presence. It is only now, man has begun to understand and appreciate the active role of the junk DNA in random generation and expression of characteristics of any individual born (see 'Junk DNA: A Journey Through the Dark Matter of the Genome' By Neesa Carey, Icon Books Ltd, 2015, and 'The Epigenetics Revolution: How Modern Biology is Rewriting Our Understanding of Genetics, Disease and Inheritance' By Neesa Carrey, Icon Books Ltd, 2012). Dr. Vidyadhar Gopal Oke, however has very rightly coined the term- "Gunarjanma" meaning the "Rebirth of Charactristic Qualities and Traits" instead of the ancient terminology of 'Rebirth".

This Chapter is based on the research paper presented at the National Conference on Ancient Science and Technology, Retrospection and Aspirations (ASTRA-2015) Fergusson College, University of Pune, January 10-11, 2015. Proceedings of the Conference, ISSN. 2321-7715. Reg. No. 67495 / 97. Academy of Sanskrit Research. Melkote-571 431.

CHAPTER 3

Work, its Origin, Kinds and the Law of Karma: A Synthesis of their Scientific Foundation and Obligations for Human Survival

3.1 Abstract

This article traces the definition and origin of perpetual work in the creation of the universe and it's various kinds in relation to the conscious life forms and human beings in particular. The origin and operation of the Universal Law of Karma has been explained on the basis of physics and modern molecular genetics. The recently discovered, perpetually ongoing process of DNA-methylation in all living organisms, which essentially defines the strategy mechanism adopted by the organism for survival under continuously changing epigenetic environmental (which include physical, physiological, terrestrial, atmospheric, cosmic and universal) conditions, has been functionally associated with the ancient, invisible mythological character called the '**Chitragupta**' since the Vedic period in India. The personified 'Chitragupta', as an assistant of Yamaraj, the deity of death, has been believed to be secretly writing detailed '**Record of all the Work Done by the Living Organism in its whole life**'. What seems astonishingly marvelous is, how the 'Rishis' from the 'Vedic Period' in India could know the subtlest function and role of the DNA molecules and their – *methylation* process as a strategy for survival by the organism under changing epigenetic environment? The ancient personified 'Chitragupta' is therefore not a myth or a concept of blind faith but a physical scientific truth. The beautiful parallel of the process of DNA-methylation, drawn in this article with the character of 'Chitragupta' who resides secretly unseen within every individual cell of the body and ceaselessly records the history of all interactions of the organism with epigenetic environment from the moment of its conception, development, birth to death, appears to be fascinating and amazingly interesting. How I wish the scientists today to look to the Vedic Philosophy from the point of view of modern science.

Introduction

3.2 Why there is perpetual work in nature?

The Universe is known to be filled with only energy and matter of various kinds, controlled by four types of natural forces, known to a physicist as; 'Weak interaction', 'Strong interaction', 'Electromagnetic' and 'Gravitation'.[1-3] Whereas only one tenth of the total matter present in the universe is visible to human eye, the balance nine tenth, continues to remain occluded and is called the dark matter or dark energy. The nature, manifestation, spread or distribution and properties of dark energy and its transformation into visible matter, continue to be a great mystery, despite tremendous progress in cosmological sciences and attempts to explain all the four natural forces by one single theory (Standard Model).[4-6] The perpetual interplay of the conversion of dark energy into visible matter and its recycling back into energy is the fundamental law of Nature. According to the modern concepts of cosmology, a Universe is believed to contain a cluster of about one hundred billion galaxies, with each galaxy consisting of about one hundred billion individual stars. And it is estimated that over a fifty orders of magnitude of this universe, lies beyond the farthest universe, visibly seen with help of most powerful telescopes located on Earth and those positioned at 540 Km above sea level in geo-stationary orbit in space, the Hubbel Space Telescope.[3-7] Light energy at its velocity of **1,86,000 miles per second** or **2,99,792.458 Km per second,** would require at least a million years to diagonally travel across any single galaxy from its one end to the other. Recent evidence gathered by the National Aeronautics and Space Administration (NASA), USA suggests that the cluster of stars within individual galaxies and galaxies across multitude of universes are not individually isolated but are mutually interconnected. **Figure 7[4] and 8** below, depict the limits of the extent of universal matter from its microscopic to the macroscopic dimensions and the physical equipments that have helped man to unfold these limits, which extend from **10^{-30} to 10^{+45} cm.** These seemingly extreme limits also represent, the extent and dimensions of human knowledge today and the human brain and mind are not only concerned with everything that lies, within these limits but are perpetually attempting to comprehend and correlate his own existence in relation to them.[1-7] However, it is clear that the key to the presence of a variety of compound matter present in the universe is the formation and availability of the lightest element i.e. Hydrogen atoms (protons) in abundance and their fusion into the formation of the other fundamental elemental atomic unit matter of about 118 different kinds, each with an individually unique mass as well as chemical, structural and physical properties.[2] And each kind of these elemental atoms, were formed in the nuclear furnaces during the formation of Stars after the singularity exploded with a 'Big Bang', approximately 14 billion years ago.[6,7] Accurate observations made with the help of the most advanced telescopes reveal that an exact balance exists between the positive energy of matter that formed and the negative energy of gravitation that immediately comes into play so that no net energy is actually required for creation of the rest of the universe.

Work, its Origin, Kinds and the Law of Karma | 91

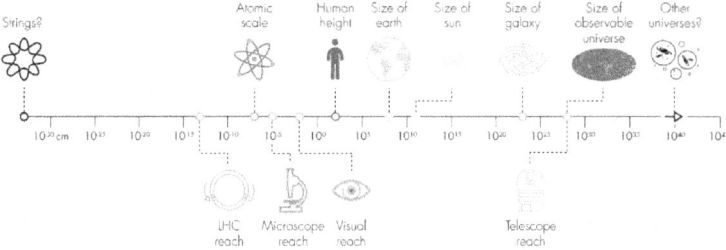

Figure 7. Dimensional limits of the extent of material and energy continuum of the universe and corresponding human knowledge today *(Reproduced with apologies from an unidentified source).*

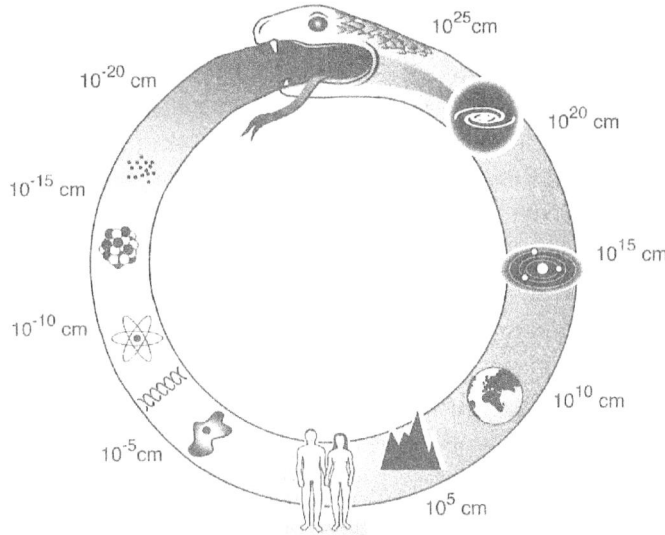

Figure 8. The ORABORUS. Indicating the connecting links between the micro-world of particles, nuclei and atoms (left) and the cosmos (right). *Reproduced here, with kind permission of the author, Lord Prof. Martin J. Rees, from his book–'Just Six Numbers', Phoenix (1999).*[4] **The illustration, as I consider, is also the pictorial representation of the factual, fundamental, Universal law of perpetual recycling of energy into matter and vice-versa in both, the inanimate (inert) and animate (living) forms of matter in nature.**

A cyclic inter-play in creation of both inanimate and animate matter and their subsequent disintegration into basic building blocks of the elemental atomic matter from which they were formed and later it's annihilation with release of considerable amounts of energy under the action of the four kinds of known forces of nature, has become the sine qua non (acquired attribute) of the manifestation of nature with all its spectacular grandeur and beauty. However, where and how, the all pervading 'consciousness' and awareness about self existence fits into this scheme of universal creation is still a mystery and the source for speculation, theories and debate. Many thinkers believe that 'Consciousness' may be the fifth force of nature but the scientists are reluctant to admit so. The other probability that has been put forward is that 'consciousness' may be a hitherto unknown and most possibly an unrecognized, collective attribute of the quantized negative or positive electric charges respectively on an electron and a proton, as a manifestation of the primordial elemental matter or energy itself. Quantized units of electric charges (on an electron or a proton) is also fundamental to both the creation and destruction of elemental matter as well as to structures of more complex nature arising out of a combination of different atoms and molecules. The life of an electron has been estimated to be 10^{66} years and is perhaps the most stable of all the elementary particles known to human beings. It may be curious to argue whether 'consciousness' exists or does not exist, at the sub-structural level (Quarks) of proton or electron and other elementary nuclear particles with fractional electric charges on them? And billions of years after his appearance on the Earth, man is still searching for scientific answers about his own consciousness, his origin, the purpose and time span of his existence. Despite these limitations, what is most evident is; that creation of matter (inanimate and animate) its sustenance for a specific predetermined period of time and its subsequent annihilation has evolved itself into a continually rhythmic, dynamic process, marked by an equilibrium in periodic cycles of energy consumption, transformation and work done against the forces of nature. Obviously therefore, performing work and accumulating that continuously in building up the potential energy has become an acquired- perpetual characteristic process in nature. Nothing can ever remain without action / work even for a fraction of a second and every inanimate and animate matter is helplessly driven to remain at work by way of its inherent qualities and natural tendencies. Whereas, progressive accumulation of potential energy, beyond limits of sustenance leads to disaster, destruction or annihilation, progressive shedding of potential energy (through personal sacrifice / inaction) leads back towards the origin and source of primordial energy or the source of consciousness.[8-14] Therefore, it is probable that a 'stimulation / initiation of some kind' similar to 'desire or urge in man' on behalf of a hitherto unknown kind of a primordial 'Force of nature' must have set the first action of transforming the abundant dark-energy into visible matter and push it into action for performing ceaseless work. The three of the four forces of nature, namely; weak interaction, strong interaction and electromagnetic, as described above, perhaps come into play, during and after the matter in its stable element form is actually created. And with the creation of mass, follows the force of gravitation. However, though difficult, the origin of the force of 'strong interaction' which binds the sub-nuclear particles together may be resulting from the stimulus received from the hitherto unknown 'Force of Nature' that provides mass to energy. The weak and strong interactive forces within the nucleus of every atom of various elements compete with the electromagnetic force for ultimate control over the atom. At times, when the strong force wins, protons and neutrons get strongly bound to produce a stable atom and when the electromagnetic force wins, it leads to an unstable entity with production of a variety of disintegrating radio- active nuclei. The Yang-Mills equation, credited to Robert Lawrence Mills and Chen Ning Yang explained the puzzling properties of subatomic particles on the basis of difference between left and right spin, when particles interact through the weak force. **Whereas electric charge is a source of an electromagnetic field, the electromagnetic field itself is not the**

source of an electric charge. Electromagnetism also does not change electric charges and the field is a source for itself by itself. Electrons were created at the time the Big Bang occurred, around 13.8 billion years ago, as energized photons interacted with each other to create an electron-positron pair. In fact, electrons are created from quarks (a fundamental sub-atomic particle). A quark is a tiny particle which makes up protons and neutrons. Atoms, in turn are made of protons, neutrons and electrons. It was once thought that all three of those were fundamental particles, which cannot be broken up into anything smaller.

Unfortunately, neither the sequence, order and process involved in the creation of electrons, protons and neutrons and assembly of nuclei of various element atoms nor the sequence in the hierarchy involved amongst the four 'forces of nature' is scientifically known to mankind. The experiments conducted with powerful atom smashing machines- the particle accelerators, have only revealed the presence of various constituent elementary particles, involved in their composition, assembly and as components but not about the process of their creation. And as long as such stimulation and recycling in converting dark energy into matter and vice versa exist, so long the perpetual performance of work (in the form of the cycle of creation and destruction) will not be over. And this cycle of creation and destruction is common to both the inanimate and animate matter because they both originate and constitute the same primordial elemental atomic material in their systems. Ever since the element atoms of 118 kinds were created at the beginning of the universe about 13.8 billion years ago, they have remained so and retained their individual identities and characteristic physical and chemical properties. In other word, all these individual element atoms of 118 kinds are the physical material entities that are conscious of their own existence, identity, capacity and properties. And since the basic element atoms are themselves being the conscious entities, a profound question that arises being; Is 'consciousness' in a living being, including humans, an attribute of collective consciousness of the billions of atoms that constitute the body parts and their mechanism?

3.3 Merging boundaries of Physics, Physical Chemistry and Biochemistry of Matter

Rupert Sheldrake [15] has recently come out with his revolutionary new concept and 'Hypothesis of Formative Causation' which states that the forms of self-organizing systems are shaped by morphic fields. Morphic fields organize atoms, molecules, crystals, organelles, cells, tissues, organs, organisms, communities, societies, ecosystems, planetary systems, solar systems and galaxies at all imaginable complexities. These morphic fields also contain an inherent memory given by the process and frequencies of morphic resonance culminating in providing each and every kind of thing a 'collective memory'. Thus, morphic fields that shape the growing biological organisms are called morphogenetic fields, in social organization they can be called social fields; and in organization of the mental activity- the mental fields. And all such kinds of fields are shaped, stabilized and act on materials to put them into perpetual work through morphic resonance. Innumerable reports from National Aeronautics And Space Administration (NASA) -USA indicate the presence of perpetual, strong geo-magnetic fields around the Earth and when a big storm of solar plasma, originating from the coronal mass ejection from the Sun, force waves of intense ionization rippling through the Earth's upper atmosphere, they cause electric currents to flow through the topsoil and shake the entire magnetic field of the planet Earth in a resonant motion and dynamic action. Whereas consciousness in the inanimate matter is considered to remain dormant but active in the animate matter for the sake of convenience, such differentiation has also been considered invalid, in view of the fact that all atoms are conscious of their own identity and existence. The so called 'Free Will' appears to be an acquired attribute of a self assembled natural or artificially assembled **'machine system'** controlled by naturally inherent or artificial intelligence for survival and work under any given epigenetic environment. And scientists consider artificially intelligent gadgets to be also conscious entities. A big boulder lying in a field does not constitute a machine and just lies there as a lump of matter. The whole universe is therefore governed by the law of perpetual work in which; action and reaction, cause and effect and effort and destiny are all equal and opposite. This law of perpetual work is 'eternal', 'universal' and 'applicable' through all the time-scales, the past, the present and the future. Conscious or unconscious defiance, ignorance of this law or willfully contravening it, leads to certain destruction. Only adherence to this law, leads to a happy and harmonious survival, irrespective of cast, creed, color of the skin, religious faith at birth and physical location anywhere in the universe.

3.4 Work, nature of work and classification of work

Perhaps the first ever definition, description, characterization and classification of work has descended down to mankind from the 'Ved and Upanishads' the philosophical texts of India and then explained in relation to personal and social behavior and human psychology in the celestial song– 'The Bhagwad Geeta'. **Karma** (car-ma) is a word meaning the combined result of a persons actions as well as the actions itself and encapsulates in it's meaning the cycle of causes and their effects.[8-14] According to **the theory of Karma**, what happens to any person happens so, because they caused it with their actions.[8-14] The simple and succinct definition of work being- 'each and every physical action, deed or movement that is performed, consciously or unconsciously, willingly or unwillingly with cooperation of the mind, using all or any of the five senses, the various organs and limbs of our body, from morning to evening, during day and night, through weeks, months, years and all through the life, from the moment of birth to the last breath, is known as 'work' or Karma. And all the work performed have been classified into three categories, (i) '**Spontaneous work**'- work done on the spur of a moment or time which bears a reaction or result almost instantaneously, (ii) '**Cumulative work**'- work done that does not produce an immediate reaction and is kept in abeyance until an opportue time arrives for the delivery of its result. No corrective measures for such actions are either available or possible, (iii) **'Previously done or accumulated work'**- work done from the 'cumulative list' in another span of time that is ready to bear results. They are also commonly described by such synonyms as 'destiny', 'luck', 'fate' and 'fortune'. Just as human beings, animals, birds, fishes or microbial life forms have different gestation time frames until birth and every different crop plant species has its own crop growth period from the sowing of seeds to harvesting, so also each and every cumulative work done in life takes a definite time for producing their consequences or results. This time period from the moment, work is done, to the delivery of its result, may be over in just one life-span or may take several hundred cycles of birth and rebirth for an individual as it is generally believed *(here cycles of birth and rebirth only mean to suggest the number of times, the self-replicating DNA molecule is multiplied with its characteristic information coded on it before completely changing and erasing the memory of any particular experience or work. Otherwise, rebirth or re-incarnation of an individual after death is scientifically and technically impossible and continues to be a mis-interpreted popular myth perpetuated over ages)*.[16,17] Rebirth or reincarnation is only possible as regeneration of the characteristic traits and attributes in a new individual born, by the routine self-replicating process of the DNA in association with its epigenetic environment and certainly not as a rebirth of an individual, once he is dead. It is in fact a *'Gunarjanma'* which is a repeated regeneration of characteristic quality traits (Guna) arising out of the cyclic self-replication of DNA under a changing epigenetic environment and not the repeated rebirth *'Punarjanma'(Janma as in birth)* of any individual after his or her death.[16-18] How, where, and in what form, the information and memory about the work done or experiences in life are recorded, stored and carried to the next birth and their consequences then encoded for execution in the new form of program loaded in the human genome-DNA, is an unresolved mystery. However, recent developments in the field of molecular genetics are gradually resolving these issues. What seems almost certain is that the human brain cannot be the vehicle or a carrier of this memory from one life to the other, although, brain is used as a tool to control and coordinate all activities in a body during life time in all animals? The phenomena appears to be working at the level of the arrangement and rearrangement of the base-pairs (Adenine, Cytosine, Thymine and Guanine, symbolized as A, C, G and T respectively) sequencing of the DNA molecules or at the sub-quantum level of an intense subtle energy or energy field, about which nothing or very little scientific knowledge is known as yet. Changes in the sequence of Base Pairs on DNA would mean a drastic change (mutation) of species itself and this appears to be impossible. However, recording of the memory of experiences suffered by any uni- or multi-cellular organism may be possible during the process of self replication of the DNA molecules and their methylation. DNA-methylation is an epigenetic mechanism used by living cells to control their gene expression. A number of other mechanisms also exist to control gene expression in eukaryotes, but DNA-methylation is a commonly used epigenetic signaling tool that can fix genes in the "off" position. Methylation is a critical process that happens trillions of times in the life time of every living cell. It is one of the most essential metabolic functions of the body and is responsible for the synthesis of a variety of enzymes and proteins, within individual cells, as a result of the stimulus received by the cell membrane from the epigenetic environment around it. Dynamically, adapting to stress and the challenges of life, arising from the sudden or gradual changes in epigenetic environment, as a strategy for survival is the essential aspect of the DNA-methylation process. Scientists have also discovered how vital the DNA-methylation is to a number of other cellular processes such as embryonic development, X-chromosome inactivation, genomic imprinting, gene suppression, carcinogenesis and chromosome stability and links of aberrations in methylation patterns to several human diseases with significant correlations. These findings could be important in aiding the development of appropriate therapies and for understanding and preventing conditions that develop right from the beginning of zygotic and embryonic development as a result of abnormal methylation of the X chromosome *(inherited either from the father or the mother)* and gene imprinting.[19,20]

DNA-Methylation does not change the existing sequence of base pairs in the DNA molecule but modifies the configuration by masking some parts of the base-pair sequences on DNA and thereby reading the coded information differently to synthesize new enzymes and proteins in accordance with this masking, during self-replication. DNA-methylation is the process through which a methyl group (- CH_3) is added to DNA nucleotides, very often to the fifth carbon atom of a cytosine ring. This conversion of cytosine bases to 5-methylcytosine is catalyzed by DNA methyltransferases (DNMTs). These modified cytosine residues usually lay next to a (G) guanine base (CpG methylation) and the result is two methylated cytosines positioned diagonally to each other on opposite strands of the DNA double helix. DNA-methylation occurs at CpG sites—i.e. the sites where a cytosine (C) is immediately in front of a guanine (G). When a CpG segment in the promoter region of a gene is methylated, the expression of the gene is suppressed (i.e. it is turned off). The extent of addition of methyl groups is controlled at several levels in cells and is carried out by a family of enzymes called DNA methyltransferases (DNMTs). Defects in DNA-methylation can result in disorders affecting embryogenesis, genomic imprinting and even the onset of cancer. The other important purpose of DNA-methylation is the formation of the chromatin structure, which enables a single cell (also called a stem cell) to grow into a complex multi-cellular organism made up of different tissues and organs.[19-22]

3.5 The New Science of Epigenetics

The science of *epigenetics* has been an associated component of the entire evolutionary process of biological life on the Earth. However, its role as an independent subject of study was established barely one and quarter century ago, almost simultaneously when the theoretical geneticists were busy in creating a dogmatic belief system that all life forms are the products of their destiny, encoded in their Genes (DNA). The immaculately crucial experiments, conducted on somatic and enucleated cells over a century ago, laid the foundation of the modern science of *epigenetics* which essentially means "control above and beyond genetics'. Three decades of research in *epigenetics* has almost established that the inherited DNA encoded blueprints at the time of birth by any life form, is certainly not its destiny! Environmental conditions such as; nutrition, physical, physiological, psychological state of the mother during intra-uterine gestation period, influence and modify inherited genes without changing their basic blueprint. And the so called 'Environment' includes grossly measurable terrestrial and atmospheric parameters, besides the subtle and almost immeasurable, cosmic and universal influences. However, in the enthusiasm of in depth studies of the DNA, the equally crucial role of chromosomal proteins in heredity was inadvertently neglected. The science of *epigenetics* is re-establishing the importance of those chromosomal proteins.[19-22]

In the chromosome, the DNA *(deoxyribonucleic acid)* forms the core, and the proteins cover this core like a sleeve. When the genes are covered, their information cannot be 'read'. In order to remove the cover off, an environmental signal is needed to spur the sleeve proteins to change their shape and get detached from the core-DNA double helix, and thereby permitting the gene to be read. Once the DNA is uncovered, the cell makes a copy of the exposed gene. The activity of the gene is thereby controlled by the presence or absence of the proteins that en-sleeved it, which in turn are controlled and regulated by the external environment. The science of *'epigenetics'* explains how environmental signals control the activity of the genes. The hitherto understood 'Primacy of the Genes' has now been revised to the 'Primacy of the Environment' and the new scheme of flow of information in cell biology, first begins with an environmental signal, passing over to the regulatory protein and only then to the *Deoxyribonucleic acid* (DNA) and *Ribonucleic acid* (RNA) and to the end product, which is also a protein. Therefore, both the two mechanisms 'genes' and 'environment' contribute equally to determining the behavior of humans and all other life forms. Thousands of variations of synthesized proteins can be produced from the same gene blueprint on DNA by environmentally controlling the regulatory proteins. And such environmentally influenced finely–tuned gene can get passed on to generation after generation. Today, the genes are now believed to be far more fluid and responsive to even minutest changes in the environment. Neither the Genes nor the cell nucleus, where they reside are now considered as the proverbial brain of the cell and control its biology. Biological cells are indeed shaped and regulated by the epigenetic environment in which they live and survive.[19-22]

3.6 The Mechanism of DNA-methylation

A series of experiments have established that 'methyl chemical group **($-CH_3$)**' is essentially involved in epigenetic modification of information encoded on the gene. When the methyl groups get attached to the DNA of a gene, they change the way the regulatory chromosomal proteins are bound to the DNA molecule. When they are bound too tight to the gene, the protein sleeve cannot be removed from over the gene to be read for transcription and multiplication. The perpetually continuous and dynamic process of 'DNA-methylation' is therefore the most essential component of any biological cell mechanism as its strategy for survival in a given environmental condition. There is convincing evidence that programming of health for entire life time of a child to be born are as much affected by the intra uterine conditions in the womb of the mother as the genes in determining our mental attitude to physical performance in life. Any modification is easy to understand when it is incorporated on the DNA itself (mutation). However, the most commonly observed modification on DNA happens when a C base is followed by a G base. This sequence is designated as CpG, and constitutes the site where enzymes secreted within cells are able to add a methyl (CH_3) group to the cystosine base. In case, a large number of CpG motifs are present in any section of DNA, a large number of methyl groups can be added epigenetically. This attracts specific proteins to the sites to repress expression of those genes. DNA methylation carried on a large number of CpG motifs lying in close proximity to each other produces exceptional effects. With methylation, the DNA changes its shape and the gene is completely switched off. And the gene remains switched off not just in that cell but in all the daughter cells that are multiplied when it divides. In case of the non-dividing cells such as the neuron cells of the brain, the patterns of DNA methylation are possibly established while a child is still in the womb of his/her mother and that pattern practically remains in place throughout the life of that child to be born. Mechanism of permanently switching genes off, during the life time of an individual through DNA methylation has provided scientists to study the root causes for the drastic variations in characteristics, behavior, attitudes, physiology, psychology and intellectual capabilities between identical paternal and monozygotic twins. Identical paternal and monozygotic twins begin to diverge epigenetically during individual development in the uterus and differ in their DNA methylation patterns. The differences between monozygotic twins become more pronounced with advancing age and exposure to different environments.

All the 30-70 trillion individual cells constituting a human body, irrespective of their function as cells of sweat gland, skin, muscle, eyelids, bone cartilage or neurons in the brain, essentially contain the same genetic code, the DNA. These specialized cells only use the information present in those genes in different ways, depending on their functional requirements. For example, in brain neuron cells, the genes responsible for producing haemoglobin are heavily methylated and they remain permanently switched off throughout life. However, in the cells that produce red blood cells, these genes are not methylated and they continue to produce haemoglobin, throughout life. Fortunately, DNA-methylation is a pretty stable configuration to keep certain genes permanently switched off. However, when our cells have to respond to short-term changes encountered in environment, they switch on to a second type of mechanism, called the 'histone protein adjustment to genes' to modulate the expression of a gene. In view of a large number of amino acids that can be modified on histone proteins and the fact that more than 60 different chemical groups can be loaded on amino acids, thousands of combinations of 'histone modifications' on the same or different genes in different cell types can be made possible. And all cells interpret these histone modifications in a different way. In a very simple language, Nessa Carrey has defined DNA-methylation as akin to the on/off switch and histone modification as the volume control.[19, 20]

Epigenetic mechanisms have also been identified to be an important factor in a variety of diseases besides cancer and cardiovascular disease and diabetes. Only 5-6% of cardiovascular and cancer patients attribute their disease to heredity, whereas ninety five percent of the breast and other cancers have been observed to be derived from the environmentally induced epigenetic alterations and certainly not because of the defective genes. Drastic changes in diet, nutrition and lifestyles of prostate cancer patients for three months or more have been found to be sufficient to switch off the activity of over 500 genes, which were responsible for the formation of their tumors. No wonder, it is here, we realize the cardinal importance of the Vedic Indian philosophical wisdom, when it calls upon human beings to be particular about their diet, nutrition and breathing.

3.7 Epigenetics in Relation to the Inherited and Accumulated Work (Karma)

Epigenetics is a rapidly developing area of human genetics and has assumed practically the same importance as the project on sequencing of the Human Genome. Science of *epigenetics*, has accelerated research into inherited (**Prarabdha-Karma**) diseases and cancer and it is anticipated that initiatives to evolve a standard definition of the 'normal human *epigenome*' *(if that should ever be possible?)* will further enhance progress towards better understanding of the role of *epigenetics* in human diseases. The sequential program of base pairs on the DNA of the sperm from the father at the time of its fertilization in the egg cell of the mother is the inherited work or the so called the *'Prarabdh Karma'* of the child to be born. Since no one can choose his or her parents for birth, there is no option but to accept the *'Prarabdh Karma'* as a continuing link with the ancestors. Unfortunately, James Watson and Francis Crick in 1953, while announcing the discovery of the double helix structure of the DNA molecule, created, a somewhat dogmatic belief system that every living organism is a product of his/her destiny and is likely to suffer as per the program encoded on the inherited DNA. Whereas, this may be partially true, the inherited DNA also gets continuously modified according to experience gained by the new-to be-born individual, right from its zygotic state, in surviving against the changing intra-uterine epigenetic environment, and continuing to do so after birth, growth, maturity to death. The survival strategy, during life cycle, is faithfully recorded on its DNA by means of the perpetual methylation process and is called the accumulated work or the *'Sanchit Karma'*. Epigenetics involves, chemical changes to DNA that prevent or enhance the reading of a base pair sequence. The precise mechanism involves, the addition of methyl groups to a gene and thereby modify, its transcription for a specific metabolic action. Early experiences recorded on our DNA not only shape our mind but they literally change how our body metabolism and physiology work at a fundamental level. Recent researches[19-21] suggest, a very strong association of significant decline in health in adulthood for a wide variety of socio-economic reasons and particularly due to poverty and mal-nutrition during childhood. And according to Professor Candace B. Pert,[23] it is the nature and amount of proteins, enzymes and hormones synthesized within the body systems that are vital for breathing, feeding, getting rid of waste, reproducing and all the other activities that characterize the living organisms. These proteins, enzymes, hormones generate and control our thoughts, induce actions and change behavior as our dynamic response to the minutest variations in epigenetic environment. The signatures of epigenetic changes have the potential to be carried on to several generations of self replications of DNA in its inheritance. The story of the revolution in epigenetic science has been beautifully discussed and documented by Nessa Carey in her two books.[19,20] Still however, approach to the subject from neurological science suggests a strong association and correlation between ultra-structural differences in the gross neuron-anatomical features of cortical symmetries or asymmetries in human brains with the display of exceptional abilities of talented individuals.

3.8 Pure and impure work

All the three categories of work have further been divided into two types; **'Pure work'** and **'Impure work'**, suggesting to mean that any work which is done, strictly in accordance with the laws of nature, is 'pure work' and that which is accomplished, either willfully or accidentally, without strictly adhering to the science involved behind the work, is called the 'impure work'. Today, if giant aeroplanes, with hundreds of human passengers or several tons of cargo, on-board are successfully flying across continents and oceans, is not because man has conquered nature but only because we are flying them strictly by adhering to and in accordance with the laws of nature, discovered by science and enable us, to do so. This is the reason, why scientists (physicists in particular) as a general rule crave, desire and work for uniform universal standards of measures for all physical quantities and for quality of materials. Further, the entire universe is well known to be rhythmic, cyclic and perfectly periodic in nature. And in keeping with this periodicity of the universe in general, cyclic nature of birth and rebirth *(as is believed for thousands of years)* is no more left to be a speculation or a fiction of blind religious faith but a scientifically established truth, governed in accordance with the 'law of work'. The only change being, that, rebirth or reincarnation taking place is not that of any individual from the historical past but it is a routine process of perpetual self-replication of the DNA molecules and near identical replication and regeneration of characteristic traits, reflected into new individuals born which includes all the uni- and multi-cellular animate life forms in nature, including plants. The DNA molecule is now believed to be constantly evolving itself by incorporating the experience gained during its interaction for survival under changing epigenetic environmental conditions by suitably changing the configuration of the sequences of base-pairs into its DNA structure and synthesis of suitable proteins as a strategy for survival of the organism. Therefore, scientifically and technically, the ancient concept of 'rebirth or reincarnation' of any individual is just impossible and continues to be a popular myth since thousands of years. The probability of near-exact replication of specific characteristics and personal traits, exhibited by an individual from the historical past, into a new born individual, at random is the only possibility left to explain our understanding about rebirth. And repeated replication and generation of specific traits under interaction with specific epigenetic environmental conditions is a routine characteristic property of the self-replicating DNA molecules. Unfortunately, such random coincidence of resemblance of characteristic traits with someone from the historical past is generally understood to be the cases of rebirth or reincarnation.[16-18] Even otherwise, for the sake of our belief in 'rebirth or reincarnation', we only compare similarities of characteristic traits, thoughts, behavior and actions and not the physical body structures, appearance or features. I am aware that under the dogmatic influence of meta-narrative books for hundreds of generations, it is not easy for any individual to dare so easily and change his / her opinion or even be receptive to a contrarian view point. This is because, practically everyone has been made to believe in the idea of rebirth by someone most revered or dear to them since their childhood. A very good compilation of comparative similarities of characteristic musical artistic excellence and traits, amongst a large number of cases of individuals, born between a wide interval of time, in India and abroad, as cases of 'plausible rebirths' has been published by Vidyadhar Gopal Oke[18]. What is satisfying to the author of this article being, that Vidyadhar Gopal Oke, has very correctly coined the term –'***Gunarjanma***'- meaning rebirth of characteristic qualities and traits (Guna) in lieu of the ancient term- *'Reincarnation or Rebirth or Punarjanma'* which has been grossly misinterpreted or misunderstood for thousands of years.[16,17]

3.9 The process of accumulating work, the 'Sanchit (accumulated) Karma', the concept of mythological character 'Chitragupta' who writes down the details of our good and bad karma done from birth to death and Human Obligations

The natural process of incorporating experiences gained by an organism on its DNA molecule, as a part of its strategy for survival in a changing epigenetic environment, by rearranging sequences of Adenosine, Thymine, Guanine and Cytosine base-pair molecules (A, T, G, C) by way of natural or artificially induced mutation, or masking certain sections of their sequence during self-replication through 'DNA-methylation' is a *de-facto* process involved in, recording experience gained by a individual cells of an organism, in dynamically adjusting internal physiology to the changing epigenetic environment outside, for their survival. This recording, of the work done, during struggle for survival is what is known as the 'accumulated work' OR the 'Sanchit Karma'. Most logically, the perpetually dynamic process of 'DNA-mythylation' going on in every individual cell of a living organism by recording the changes in its epigenetic environment and corresponding synthesis of essential enzymes, hormones and proteins as a strategy for survival,[19-21] may in fact be corresponding to the concept of **'Chitragupta'**, **(Figure 9)**[22] the Indian mythological Assistant of 'Yamaraj' the Deity of death. 'Chitragupta', as an integral functionary of the Deity of Death, has been assigned the task of keeping an in-depth track record of all the good and bad work (good or aberrant mutations or methylations) done by the living organisms, from their birth to death and help Yamaraj in deciding the fate of all that work for the future. According to a fascinating and perhaps prophetic legend in India, 'Chitragupt', was secretly (Gupt) conceived and mentally pictured (Chitra) by the creator of the Universe – 'Bramha' in its mind as a humanlike figure holding a paper and an ink-pot in his hands with a sword girdled to his waist. He was therefore named as 'Chitragupta' and empowered to dispense justice and punish those who violated the 'Dharma', which means the natural scientific laws for survival in doing their work and not any religion or religious belief. Curiously enough and quite logically, the ink-pen in the hand of Chitragupta suggests to the record of dynamically changing epigenetic environment around the organism that triggers rewriting, modification or masking of the genetic information on the DNA molecules, and onset of metabolic sequential events within cells in consequence.

Figure 9. Symbolic Idol of 'Chitragupta' holding a pen made of peacock feather and an ink pot in his left hand. As Assistant of Lord Yama the deity of death, Chitragupta has the mandate to keep writing the details of Karma using his pen till there is ink in the inkpot and thereafter use his sword to strike death. *(Reproduced from Home/devotional/ Chitragupta Maharaj (Lord Chitragupta) Best and Beautiful hd wallpapers/photos free down load, April 17, 2019 from the web)*[22]

And obviously, the symbolic 'paper' in the hands of 'Chitragupta' is this writing of the record of the 'work' through the 'DNA-methylation' process. Once methylation is completed, the organism undergoes its life according to the new sequential program encoded on the DNA. **Therefore, work, its nature, cause and effects have a continuing link to the genetic make-up of the DNA molecules.**[20,21] And specific characteristic traits, qualities, physique, physiology and psychology of the new individual born would be the reflection of new set of proteins synthesized in accordance with the modified sequence of its DNA. Such changes, though incredibly small have profound implications on the overall personality of any individual. What is certain being that every work done *(considered here only in respect of human beings for obvious reasons)* will have its reaction, every cause will have its effect and every effort done has its destiny within a time frame which is specific to the kind and nature of the work done. **It is in keeping with this truth, that every human being is born with individual specific characteristic traits, potential, capacity and ability for specific kind and nature of his 'delineated work'.**[16-21] Not only this, but nature has also provided to every individual born as a human being, an opportunity to wipe out or correct the results of the cumulative work encoded on his DNA through his/her focused conscious efforts in rearranging the sequenced program. And this is achievable with conscious regular practice of controlling breath, mind and thoughts. Our, success, personal satisfaction and salvation lie only in identifying and recognizing our 'nature-delineated' work, understanding the responsibilities involved in doing our delineated work and performing that to the best of our potential, capacity and ability. This is indeed the secret of all those successful people in any society, anywhere in the world. Complexities arise because of incorrect recognition and the choices made in choosing the nature and kind of delineated work under incorrect guidance, emotion, coercion, compulsion, intimidation, threat, perceived greed for monetary gain and desire or for any such reasons. Whereas, the compromise so made under any such circumstances might successfully provide education, employment and sufficient livelihood to an individual for life but not the inherent satisfaction of personal accomplishment. No wonder, innumerable individuals can be found in any society all over the world, willingly pursuing entirely different work than what they were educated and trained for. **What seems to be marvelous is, how the 'Rishis' from the Vedic Period in India could have conceived, understood and personified the concept and functions of 'Chitragupta' which is akin to the function of the process of 'DNA-methylation' discovered by the modern science of molecular genetics and its fundamental role in the life of any living organism.**[22]

The truth in this fact can be best realized through individual introspection and personal experiences rather than through a debate. Personal experiences very often become the determinant of the personal convictions in regard to the performance of the delineated work. Unfortunately, academic universities in most countries, instead of restricting their role in moulding philosophers and thinkers and engaging primarily in creating new knowledge, are taking upon themselves, the role of running training schools for job and employment-oriented professional trades for commercial reasons. This activity should have best been left exclusively to the polytechnics or technical schools meant for the purpose.

3.10 Natural delineation of work, their signals and responsibility of parents

The implications of work, therefore, are not only linked to the very creation of the universe but extend to everything that forms a part of the universe. The entire universe is governed by the 'Law of Karma', which is absolutely impersonal, incorruptible, beyond manipulation and free from any intervention. There is therefore no option before human beings but to submit and accept what is offered to them by the nature. And this offer comes to human beings as signal-indications in the form of inherent abilities such as; natural aptitude, inclination for certain kinds of work, inner urge, compulsive self motivation, convictions, dedication, determination, independent thinking and inherent will to perform, sharp memory, alertness, keen observation, ability to quickly grasp specific knowledge, open and receptive mind and will to change without bias or prejudice. These attributes provide the necessary guide to seek, accept and complete the delineated work. Successful parenthood therefore lies in recognizing such indications in their children and in providing all necessary help to them in making the correct choice.

3.11 Interdependence for work in societies and division of labour

The fundamental periodic re-cycling characteristic of nature is clearly evident from the fact that one kind of life-form is a food for the survival of the other kind of life as a part of the food-chain. What is excreted by one life-form as waste becomes the food for survival of the other. In this process, what each form of life is factually doing being; it is picking up the atoms and molecules of the basic food-elements which are essentially required to maintain the biochemical, physiological and physical functions of its own body for healthy existence as an individual. And since the elements so essentially required for our existence are cosmic in origin, all life forms are indirectly linked to the cosmic universe.

Like the component interdependence in a food chain, human society is also interdependent on a number of individuals who carry out many types of physical, intellectual and social work for its requirement as a group, community or a nation. In this spirit of interdependence, upholding the dignity of labor, it is totally wrong to claim or maintain superiority or inferiority of one kind of job over the other. All kinds of jobs (work) are complementary and equally important. It is the disproportionate monetary pay structures devised by the humans or unavoidable dirtying hands in doing some kind of jobs that have created such social divide. However, irrespective of any country, community, society and civilization in the history and at present, allotment of work to individuals has actually been based on mental, intellectual and physical capacity of each individual. In the absence of regular training schools in large numbers in the historical past, useful practical trades were handed down from the forefathers and parents to the children through generations. Carrying forward this tradition of work with conviction and motivation by children used to become means of his inward advancement, improvement, improvisation, innovation, research and development. No wonder all this lead to the establishment of family trades and professions. Such families pursuing different trades without rivalry or jealousy complemented each other and helped in maintaining a harmonious society at large. Today, with development of science and technology, the number of new practical trades and professions for livelihood has multiplied thousand fold. It is practically impossible to expect people to stick to the traditional family-trades under the changed scenario. Despite these developments and changes, the fundamental natural 'Law of Work' stays inviolate. People in all societies, communities and countries, consciously or unconsciously, continue to still get classified / segregated into four type of job categories, namely; (i) those that are creating new knowledge (ii) those that help in protecting the society interests (iii) those who venture into trading and transport of essential commodities for the society and (iv) those, who help in maintaining cleanliness, community hygiene and environmental aesthetics. Today, the number of various kinds of jobs falling within each of the above category has increased with technological and industrial progress. However, such classification actually evolves and comes out more from the inherent inclination, temperament, aptitude or compulsions arising out of the actions on the part of the individual himself, strictly in accordance with the 'Law of Work' than merely from inheritance and birth. Every individual is responsible himself for the kind of job that comes to his fold and no body else can be held responsible. Fortunately, under the current economic scenario, each one of us is expected to routinely perform all the four types of jobs for himself / herself, if not for others.

3.12 Ethical and moral obligations in performance of work

Having been pushed into doing our delineated work, it becomes our duty to carry out the same with utmost capacity, ability and sincerity. Any negligence in doing that work gets reflected in consequences that befall on the society besides disrupting the entire chain of interdependent community life. Therefore, creating sensitivity, sensibility and preparing mind-set in moulding young generation since childhood for a disciplined and duty-bound community life, becomes the primary responsibility of parents at home and teachers in schools and should form the first lessons of the beginning of a formal education. The level of discipline becomes more and more rigorous with progress in education and higher responsibilities of work. And surely, this is impossible to handle and carry forward without adhering to the 'laws of nature' and the 'law of work'. Craving and working for reward and recognition for doing the 'delineated work', tantamount to bargain and is a sign of an individual with a weak mind, lacking self-esteem and respect. At the same time a judicious, responsible and responsive authority is ever expected to identify, recognize and encourage good worker and good piece of work done. Conflicts arise when exploitation for gain and profit overrides all other considerations due to systemic deficiencies, subversions, sabotage or collective failure on the part of community to check such malaise.

Dictionaries describe 'ethics' as a science of moral principles or moral duty and 'morality' as concerned with right or wrong conduct in practicing virtue. Ethical and moral conduct in human behaviour, though complex, is certainly not exclusive to him / her because all forms of living creatures exhibit practicing their ethical and moral responsibilities in raising, rearing, feeding and protecting their progenies to their best of capacity until the progenies are on their own. And such other responsibilities as keeping vigil and protection against natural predators, hunting in groups and sharing food etc. are carried out by them both individually and collectively in groups or herds. The performance of work on ethical basis is not comparable to 'duty-bound' work done. The concept of 'ethics' lays more in human imagination and cannot possibly be generalized as being common in all living organisms.

3.13 Obligations, responsibilities and conduct for scientists

Scientists from all disciplines, all nationalities and communities have been individually and collectively responsible for the material progress made and comforts provided to human kinds. They not only create new knowledge but transform that into useful products for mass production, consumption, use and comfort thereby containing or at least restraining jealousies, rivalries amongst populace who have and have-not. However, it is the sagacity and responsibility of the knowledgeable, sagacious, enlightened and the ruling class of human beings to exploit new knowledge for the benefit and welfare of masses and curb the destructive / harmful use of the same. **Almost all scientists pursue science essentially to satisfy their intellectual curiosity.** They propose hypothesis without parochialism, blind-beliefs and work hard to seek evidence for or against the hypothesis. A meager piece of new information discovered can be a starting point for a new industry and provides enough excitement and inspiration to them to continue their pursuit. In the olden days, scientists in general used to avoid or hide curiosity in public, about investigations in the fields such as; spirituality, mind, the aura fields, morphic and morphogenetic fields, paranormal, psychokinetic, consciousness, out of body experiences or even life after death phenomena for they were considered to be out of scientific culture for investigation. However, the rise and growth of 'Quantum Physics', 'Theory of Relativity', elementary particle physics and cosmology and their implications in understanding the nature of reality, have demolished all barriers, inhibitions, skepticism, reservations, prejudices, biases and dogmas in the study of these or related phenomena as problems of scientific inquiry. **A true-scientist is therefore expected to be open to every kind of possibility** and approaches to solving a particular problem in a multi-disciplinary effort. **He should not be averse to considering every possible idea, how so ever bizarre it might appear, just because there is no precedent investigation reported on this line of approach.** Today, any kind of scientific enquiry, starting from any discipline converges at the end on the ultimate nature of realty, the consciousness and its manifestation. Therefore, scientists are best advised to remain aware of the spectacular revolutionary developments in physics besides confining themselves to their own branch of science. After all physics and its laws form the under current of all scientific investigations. Who knows, carrying new ideas from seemingly unrelated discipline to your own may provide new understanding in your field of investigation? What is important being to keep the flame of inner urge and passion for new knowledge constantly burning within the heart, without fear, bias, prejudice and pride? One of the most successful public educators Mr. Shiv Khera maintains- "Winners don't do different things, they do things differently". Lord Krishna in the 'Srimad Bhagwad Geeta' also pronounces *"Yogah Karmasu Koushalam"*, meaning "Any work accomplished to perfection with utmost sincerity and to the best of one's ability is Yoga".

References

Chapter 1

1. Vartak, P.V., (1999) 'The Scientific Dating of the Ramayana & Vedas' Ved Vidnyan Mandala, Vartak Ashram, 497, Shaniwar Peth, Pune, 411030, India.pp.
2. Vartak, P.V. (2012) 'Upanishadanchey Vidnyan-Nishtha Nirupan' Vol. 1, 6 th edition, In Marathi, Vartak Ashram, 497, Shaniwar Peth, Pune, 411030, India.
3. Vartak, P.V. (2013) 'Upanishadanchey Vidnyan-Nishtha Nirupan' Vol. 2, 6 th edition, In Marathi, Vartak Ashram, 497, Shaniwar Peth, Pune, 411030, India.
4. Morgia, James V. (2001)'The Mighty Electron Recycles All' Trafford Publishing.
5. Weiss, Brian, (1988) 'Many Lives Many Masters' A Fireside Book, Published by Simon & Schuster.
6. Ross, Elizabeth Kubler (2008) On Life After Death' New Foreword by Caroline Myss, Celestial Arts- An Imprint of Speed Press.
7. Ross, Elizabeth Kubler (1998) 'The Wheel of Life: A Memoire of Living and Dying' A Touchstone Book, published by Simon and Scribner. Pp.286.
8. Weaver, Richard F. (2008) 'We Are Our Ancestors', Rosedog Books. Pp 156.
9. Sheldrake, Rupert (1995) 'A New Science of Life-The Hypothesis of Morphic Resonance', Park Street Press, Rochester, Vermont. pp.
10. Sheldrake, Rupert (2012) 'The Science Delusion-Freeing the Spirit of Enquiry' Coronet.
11. Sheldrake, Rupert (2011) 'The Presence of the Past: Morphic Resonance and the Habits of Nature', Icon Books, London.
12. Dawkins, Richard (2007) ' The God Delusion' Black Swan, U.K. Page 283.
13. Hinde, Robert (1999) 'Why Gods Persist- A Scientific Approach to Religion', Routledge, pp. 304.
14. Weiss, Brian L., (1988) 'Many Lives, Many Masters', A Fireside book, pages 35-36.

15. Home Page of Edgar Cayce' A.R.E., Association for Research and Enlightenment' 215, 67 th Street, Virginia Beach, VA 23451 pp.
16. Thakkar, Hirabhai (2001) 'Theory of Karma' Kusum Prakashan, Ahmedabad, India.
17. Frank-Kamenetskii and Maxim D. (1977) Biophysics of DNA Molecule, Physics Reports, 288, 13-60.
18. Moharir, A.V. (2015) Questions about Soul and Rebirth : Need for a Fresh Look and Redefinition. Paper presented at the National Conference on Ancient Science and Technology ; Retrospection and Aspirations (ASTRA-2015), Fergusson College, University of Pune, Maharashtra, India, January 10-11, 2015. Proceedings of the Conference, ISSN- 2321-7715, Reg. No. 67495/97, Academy of Sanskrit Research, Melkote-571431, India.
19. Swaab, Dick, Frans (2014) We are our brains: From the womb to Alzheimer's" Translated By Jane Hedley-Prole, Penguine Books.
20. Atkins Peter, Reactions : The Private life of atoms, Oxford University Press
21. Warder, George Woodyard (1903) The Universe a Vast Electric Organism. ISBN-13: 978-0554494760 and ISBN-10: 0554494760.
22. Chown, Marcus (2000) 'The Magic Furnace-The Search for the Origins of Atoms' Vintage.
23. Eroglu, Halit, (2012),'The Theory of Everything', An English translation of the revised and expanded third edition of the work- "Die Weltformel-Die Urkraft des Universums". e-Book, www.hc10.ed, ISBN 978-3-8442-3885-3.
24. Vartak, P.V.,(2012) Fifth Edition, 'Bramharshinchee Smaran Yatra' An Autobiography (In Marathi), Adhyatma Sanshodhan Mandir,Vartakashram, 497, Shaniwar Peth, Pune, India.
25. Prabhupada, Swami Bhaktivedanta, A.C. (2010) Seventeenth Edition, 'Easy Journey to Other Planets', The Bhaktivedanta Book Trust, Mumbai, India.
26. Satyananda Saraswati Swami (2013 Golden Jubilee Edition) Kundalini Tantra, Yoga Publication Trust, Munger, Bihar, India. Pages
27. Naamam Ron(2015) Biological Molecules Select their Spin, Nancy & Stephen Grand Research Center for Sensors and Security, Weizmann Institute.
28. Mee, Nicholas, (2012) 'Higgs Force : Cosmic Symmetry Shattered, The Story of the greatest scientific discovery of fifty years' Quantum Wave Publishing.

29. Lipton, Bruce H.(2005), 'The Biology of Belief-Unleashing the power of Consciousness, Matter and Miracles', Hay House, pp 202.
30. Lanza, Robert (2013) The American Scholar: A New Theory of the Universe the American scholar.org/a-new-theory-of-the-universe/
31. Lanza, Robert and Bob Berman (2009) 'Biocentrism' How Life and Consciousness are the Keys to Understanding the True Nature of the Universe. Benbella Books, Dallas, TX. *(See also the website of Professor Robert Lanza for details at (http://www.robertlanzabiocentrism.com)*
32. Dawkins, Richard (2006) The Selfish Gene, Oxford University Press, UK.
33. Vartak, P.V. (2012) 7 th edition, 'Swayambhu', In Marathi, Published By Mrs. Shobhana P. Vartak, 521, Shaniwar Peth, Pune-411030, India.
34. Vartak, P.V. (2012) 2 nd edition, 'Vaidic Vidnyan Va Ved-kaal Nirnay', In Marathi, Vartak Publications, Vartakashram, 497, Shaniwar Peth, Pune-411030, India.
35. Knapp, Stephen, (2014) 'The Greatness of Ancient India's Developments', Asian Agri-History, Vol. 18, No. 2, 167-177.
36. Waradpande, N.R. The Three Editions of Mahabharata, Free-Download from the website of the author <www.nrwaradpande.in>.
37. Ashcroft, Frances, 'The Spark of Life'(2012) Penguin Books.
38. Zhou, Shu-Ang and Mitsuru Uesaka (2006) Bioelectrodynamics in living organisms, International Journal of Engineering Science, 44, 67-92, Elsevier <www.elsevier.com/locate/ijengsci>.
39. Ho, Mae-Wan (2008) 'The Rainbow and the Worm: The Physics of Organisms' World Scientific, pp380.
40. Institute of Science in Society (ISIS) Report 04/02/13. Life is Water Electric, ISIS website archieved by the British Library as UK national documentary heritage.
41. Clegg, Brian (2012) The Universe Inside You: The extreme science of the human body from quantum theory to the mysteries of the brain, Icon Books Ltd. London, UK.
42. Ashcroft, Frances, (2012) The Spark of Life: Electricity in the human body, Penguin Books.
43. Pert, Candace B., (1997) 'Molecules of Emotion', Pocket Books, London.
44. Cochran, A.A., (1971) 'Relationships between quantum physics and biology', Foundations of Physics, Vol. 1, No. 03, pp 235-250.

45. Neilsen, Mark T., Ions: The Body's Electrical Energy Source, Professor, Department of Botany, University of Utah.
46. Vartak, P.V. (2012) 6 th Edition, 'Poonarjanma' in Marathi, Published by the author, 521, Shaniwar Peth, Mehunpura, Pune, 411030, India. pp 304.
47. Pagel, Heinz R. (1982) 'The Cosmic Code-Quantum Physics as the Language of Nature', Penguine Books.
48. Singh, T.D. (Bhaktiswarupa Damodara Swami), (2002) 'Vedanta and Science-1, Human Life and Evolution of Consciousness', Savijnanam, Journal of Bhaktivedanta Institute, Vol.1, 51-74.
49. Hey, Tony (Antony) and Patrick Walters (2003) 'The New Quantum Universe' Cambridge University Press. Pp 268-283.
50. Goswami, Amit (2001) 'Physics of the Soul: The Quantum Book of Living, Dying, Reincarnation and Immortality', Hampton Roads Publishing Company, pp 288.

The following three books have also been of invaluable help to the author in understanding the concepts of energy, soul, kundalini, nadis and swarodaya vidnyan in a holistic way.

1. Annonymous, 'Yog Vidnyan' Vol. 1 (2014) and Vol. 2 (2011), Shri Pitambara Peeth, Datia, Madhya Pradesh, India.
2. Annonymous, 'Swaroday- Vidnyan' (2003) Shri Peetambara Peeth Sanskrit Parishad, Datia, Madhya Pradesh, India.
3. The Energy of Life : The science of what makes our minds and bodies work By Guy Brown, (2000) The Free Press.

Chapter 2

1. Vartak, P.V., (1999) 'The Scientific Dating of the Ramayana & Vedas' Ved Vidnyan Mandala, Vartak Ashram, 497, Shaniwar Peth, Pune, 411030, India.
2. Vartak, P.V. (2012) 'Upanishadanchey Vidnyan-Nishtha Nirupan' Vol. 1, 6 th edition, In Marathi, Vartak Ashram, 497, Shaniwar Peth, Pune, 411030, India.
3. Vartak, P.V. (2013) 'Upanishadanchey Vidnyan-Nishtha Nirupan' Vol. 2, 6 th edition, In Marathi, Vartak Ashram, 497, Shaniwar Peth, Pune, 411030, India.
4. Osborn, David H. (2009-2010) 'Science of the Sacred' LuLu.com Publishers, pdf copy available on net.

5. Vartak, P.V.,(2012) 'Poorarjanma' 6 th Edition, Published by the Author, 521, Shaniwar Peth, Pune-411030, India.
6. Weiss, Brian, (1988) 'Many Lives Many Masters'A Fireside Book, Published by Simon & Schuster.
7. Ross, Elizabeth Kubler (2008) On Life After Death' New Foreword by Caroline Myss, Celestial Arts- An Imprint of Speed Press.
8. Ross, Elizabeth Kubler (1998) 'The Wheel of Life: A Memoire of Living and Dying' A Touchstone Book, published by Simon and Scribner. Pp.286.
9. Weaver, Richard F. (2008) 'We Are Our Ancestors', Rosedog Books. pp 156.
10. Moharir, A.V.,(2014) 'A Scientific Look at the Soul: An Attempted Synthesis', 'University News'-A Weekly Journal of Higher Education, Published by the Association of Indian Universities, New Delhi, Vol. 52, No. 29, July 21-27, pp 19-30. Also Presented at the 88 th Session of Indian Philosophical Congress, S V University, Tirupati, Andhra Pradesh, India, October 17-19, 2014.
11. Cochran, A.A., (1971) 'Relationships between quantum physics and biology', Foundations of Physics, Vol. 1, No. 03,pp 235-250.
12. Pert, Candace B., (1997) 'Molecules of Emotion: Why You Feel the Way You Feel' Pocket Books, London, Sydney, New York, Toronto.
13. Vartak, P.V.,(2011) 'Yugapurush Shri Krishna' 2 nd Edition, In Marathi, Vartak Prakashan, Vartakashram, 497, Shaniwar Peth, Pune-411030, India
14. Osho, (2014), ''Dhyan Yog-Mool Sandesh' Abstracted article from the book-Mana Hee Pooja, Mana Hee Dhoop' in Hindi, Osho World, December Issue, pp 16-18.
15. Zukav, Gary, (1989) 'The Seat of the Soul' Rider, Random House Books, London, Sydney,Auckland, Johhanesberg.
16. Guney, M.R., (2005) 'Geetartha Vishwa" In Marathi, Snehal Prakashan, Pune, India, pp 112-113.
17. Kak, Subhash, (2006) 'Garbha Upanishad: Translation and Notes', Published by the author.
18. Thakkar, Hirabhai (2001) 'Theory of Karma' Kusum Prakashan, Ahmedabad, India.
19. Sheldrake, Rupert (1995) 'A New Science of Life-The Hypothesis of Morphic Resonance', Park Street Press, Rochester, Vermont. pp.
20. Sheldrake, Rupert (2012) 'The Science Delusion-Freeing the Spirit of Enquiry' Coronet.

21. Sheldrake, Rupert (2011) 'The Presence of the Past: Morphic Resonance and the Habits of Nature', Icon Books, London.
22. Sheldrake, Rupert (2011) 'Dogs That Know When Their Owners are Coming Home, and Other Unexplained Powers of Animals', Three River Press.
23. Osho-Rajnish, 'Gita Darshan', Vol-1, Discourse 8, Abridged in the Cover Story, 'Vidyut Kanon se Nirmeet Shareer' in Hindi, published in 'Osho World', January 2015.
24. Steinheimer, Joel, http://www.earthpulse.com / science / songs.html
25. Schrodinger, Erwin, (1955) 'What is Life' Cambridge University Press.
26. Lipton, Bruce H.(2005), 'The Biology of Belief-Unleashing the power of Consciousness, Matter and Miracles', Hay House, pp 202.
27. Lanza, Robert (2013) The American Scholar: A New Theory of the Universe theamericanscholar.org/a-new-theory-of-the-universe.
28. Lanza, Robert and Bob Berman (2009) 'Biocentrism' How Life and Consciousness are the Keys to Understanding the True Nature of the Universe. Benbella Books, Dallas, TX. *(See also the website of Professor Robert Lanza for details at http://www.robertlanzabiocentrism.com)*
29. Ashcroft, Frances, 'The Spark of Life'(2012) Penguine Books.
30. Pagel, Heinz R. (1982) 'The Cosmic Code-Quantum Physics as the Language of Nature', Penguine Books
31. Ho, Mae-Wan (2008) 'The Rainbow and the Worm: The Physics of Organisms' World Scientific, pp380.
32. Hey, Tony (Antony) and Patrick Walters (2003) 'The New Quantum Universe' Cambridge University Press. Pp 268-283.
33. Goswami, Amit (2001) 'Physics of the Soul: The Quantum Book of Living, Dying, Reincarnation and Immortality', Hampton Roads Publishing Company, pp 288.

Chapter 3

1. Rousseau Pierre., 'From Atom to Star', S Chand & Co. 1987, pp78.
2. Emsley, John., 'Nature's Building Blocks- An A-Z Guide to the Elements, Oxford University Press, 2001, pp539.
3. Hey, Tony and Walters Patrick., 'The New Quantum Universe' Cambridge University Press, 2004, pp357.
4. Rees Martin., 'Just Six Numbers', Phoenix (1999).
5. Weinberg, Steven., 'The Discovery of Subatomic Particles, Cambridge University Press (2003).

6. Stenger, Victor J., 'The Comprehensible Cosmos : Where Do the Laws of Physics Come From?, Prometheus Books (2006).
7. Weinberg, Steven., 'The First Three Minutes : A Modern View of the Origin of the Universe' Basic Books (1993).
8. Guney, M.R., 'Dynaneshwari chey Bhava Vishwa' in Marathi, Snehal Prakashan, Pune, 2006, pp192.
9. Guney, M.R., 'Geetartha Vishwa' in Marathi (annotated with Commentary and translation in English by the author himself), Snehal Prakashan, Pune, 2005, pp 297.
10. Athaley, Keshav Ganesh., Critical Commentary on Shri Dasbodh by Samartha Swami Ramdas, 'Shri Dasbodh-Gudhartha Deepika' in Marathi, Shri Dasbodh Gudhartha Deepika Prakashan Mandal, Indore & Ujjain, India, 1993, pp.710.
11. Vivekananda, Swami., 'Karma Yog' Ramakrishna Mission
12. Pujyashri Chandrasekharendra Sarasvatisvamigal., Shankaracharya of Kanchi Kamakoti Peetha., 'Hindu-Dharma-The Universal Way of Life-Voice of the Guru', Bharatiya Vidya Bhavan, Bombay, 1995, pp 790.
13. 'Eight Upanishads', Vol.1 (Isa, Kena, Katha and Taittiriya), Translated by Swami Gambhiranand., Advaita Ashram, Calcutta, 1972, pp 408.
14. Thakkar, Hirabhai., 'Theory of Karma' English Translation of original in Gujrati, Kusum Prakashan, Ahmedabad, India, 2001,pp 80.
15. Sheldrake, Rupert., 'The Hypothesis of A New Science of Life-Morphic Resonance', Park Street Press, 1995, pp 272.
16. Moharir, Anil Vishnu., 'A Scientific Look at the Concept of Soul: An Attempted Synthesis', Zorba Books, Gurugram, 2017. And
17. Moharir, Anil Vishnu., 'Questions about Soul and Rebirth: Need for a Fresh Look and Re-definition', Paper Presented at the National Conference on Ancient Science and Technology, Retrospection and Aspirations (ASTRA-2015) Fergusson College, University of Pune, January 10-11, 2015. Proceedings of the Conference, ISSN. 2321-7715. Reg. No. 67495 / 97. Academy of Sanskrit Research. Melkote-571 431.
18. Oke, Vidyadhar Gopal., 'Punarjanma : Mithya ki Tatthya' in Marathi (Reincarnation : Myth or Truth', Param Mitra Publications, Thane, Maharashtra, India, 2018, pp 259.
19. Nessa Carey., 'The Epigenetic Revolution : How Modern Biology is Rewriting our Understanding of Genetics, Disease and Inheritance' Icon Books Ltd, 2012, pp 339.

20. Nessa Carey., 'Junk DNA : A Journey Through the Dark Matter of the Genome' Icon Books Ltd, 2015, pp340.
21. Lipton, Bruce H., 'Biology of Belief : Unleashing the Power of Consciousness, Matter & Miracles', Hay House, 2008.
22. Home/devotional/Chitragupta Maharaj (Lord Chitragupta) Best and Beautiful hd wallpapers/photos free down load, April 17, 2019 from the web).
23. Pert, Candace B., Molecules of Emotion: Why You Feel the Way You Feel, Pocket Books, 1997.

Appendix 1
Abstract on the first edition of the book with views and comments received

This book traces the developments in efforts and difficulties encountered in understanding the enigmatic concept of Soul and rebirth being discussed for over 5,000 years of human history and yet being far away from consensus. The reasons are more of religious dogma, divide, blind faith and above all; fear and lack of courage on the part of people to cross the religious and social barriers arising out from the teaching, interpretations and dogma of 'meta-narrative' books to rebel in favour of scientific logic, arguments and truth. Despite developments in material sciences, elementary particle physics, space science and technology and molecular biology, our understanding of the concept of Soul, its meaning, nature, constitution, structure, function and physical location within body in relation to environment, physiology, psychology, biochemistry, thought process, nature of memory and physical behavior are still not known holistically. The author argues against the old concept of 'Soul' taking its permanent residence within the body of an organism from the moment of birth to its death. It has instead been argued that the so called 'Soul' actually remains in continual connection with the universal consciousness (electric potential continuum) from the moment of conception, development, birth to until death through 'electric charge' mediated within millions of ion channels in bodies of living organisms. Whenever the physical body of any living organism from the unicellular bacteria to the most evolved of all species the human being is incapacitated for a sustained flow of electric charge / universal consciousness / ionic movements within itself to drive electric currents through ion-channels in motivating the conscious body, death occurs. Therefore, death of any organism is not an instantaneous process but a gradual progressive closing of ion-channels from various organs and parts in a sequential order. The Vedic concept and structural model for the Soul, described about 8,000 years BC, has been described and logically discussed in relation to the developments in science and known facts about life to assert that everything attributed to and described about the qualities, properties and characteristics of 'Soul' are also true about 'Electric Charge'. Therefore, there is merit in assuming that under dogmatic influences of religious beliefs, descended down to us through hundreds of centuries, we have perhaps lost courage to introspect and failed to recognize 'Electric Charge' to be the de-facto 'Soul' that drives the entire living world irrespective of its terrestrial, aquatic or plant origins. The book is not a narrative on metaphysical entities such as 'soul' or 'rebirth' but a multidisciplinary synthesis to assert, that what we have been assuming to be metaphysical for centuries in the past are in fact physical entities. Still however, until a global consensus is built up on the expressed views on scientific merits, the Vedic concept of Soul stands tall and provides a logical, quasi-scientific explanation to satisfy human curiosity. The task of compiling a comprehensive multidisciplinary review article with a purely scientific outlook about such a complex subject as 'Soul' was a daunting task. Moreover, it is very difficult to expect a uniformly common multi-disciplinary background from all readers besides willingness to welcome and consider radical thoughts. Still, it is hoped that the readers would appreciate the efforts with an open mind and read something unconventional. Not only this, but as I hope, readers would muster courage to look to our ancient concepts with renewed curiosity and with an unbiased / unprejudiced mind. *The discoverer of the structure of the DNA, Sir Francis Crick had observed- "Now is the time to think scientifically about consciousness (and its relationship, if any to the hypothetical immortal soul) and most important of all, the time to start the experimental study of consciousness in a serious deliberate way."* **And the present book fulfills the desire expressed by Sir Francis Crick in perhaps the best possible way to date.**

Foreword to the book has been written by **Prof. Dr. Ravin Lakshman Thatte,** MS, FRCS (EDIN), Renowned and pioneering Plastic and Reconstructive Surgeon, author and profound writer from Mumbai. He is also an authority on the interpretation of "Shrimad Bhagwad Gita" and "Dnyaneshwari" by Sant Dnyaneshwar, a twelth century poet philosopher.

Some Comments Received from Readers of the first edition of this book

"I wish him (A. V. Moharir) a long and healthy life so that he contributes to the well being of humanity. Naturally he will dispel misconceptions about religious entities like Soul as he has in his book- A Scientific Look at the Concept of Soul: An Attempted Synthesis. **I am in perfect agreement with what he has written in this book. This book will help removal of peoples' misconceptions about topics like - Soul, God, Heaven, Rebirth and so on, much to increase the rational happiness of humanity.**-- *Professor Dr. D. D. Bandiste, Professor of Philosophy (Retired), 148, Indrapuri Colony, Indore, M.P. PIN – 452001.*

"**I resonate with the tenor of your book and the ideas expressed in your article,** particularly the Vedic view of the structure and composition of 'Soul' " --*Joachim Keppler, Ph.D., DIWISS / Consciousness Research, Markgraffenstrasse 2, 91154 Roth, Germany.*

"We have received it. **It seems like a very beautiful piece of work on the nature of 'Soul'.** Our Secretary has presented it to His Holiness and explained a little about its content. **His Holiness thanks you for your gesture and said that it is an innovative way to look at the concept and could be helpful to those in the field of philosophy and religion.**" --*Mr Tenzin Sherab, Special Assistant to H.H. The Dalai Lama, Dharamshala, Himachal Pradesh, India.*

"**It is a great attempt to synthesize a very difficult topic. Your claim, that rebirth of a physical body is merely a random recycling of DNA and new combination of natural elements of energy is correct.** It can be considered as multiple rebirths of which one such combination may resemble the previous body." --*Mr Ramesh V. Date, Pune, Maharashtra.*

"**Heartiest congratulations for your new publication. You have entered a field which is boundless.** I hope you will further explore the mysteries of body, soul, mind and spirit in your forthcoming volumes." --*Dr. Ranjan R. Kelkar*, *Director General (Retired,) India Meteorological Department, Pune, Maharashtra, India*

"**In the mind of this reviewer, Dr. Moharir might be introducing an entirely new branch of philosophy to the existing schools.** In this small book, Dr. Moharir has proposed four new premises and has logically discussed them in the light of modern theories and with the Standard Model of Elementary Particle Physics. They are: (a) the hitherto enigmatic 'Soul' is nothing else but the *de facto* primal electric charge. (b) Souls of all living organisms remain in continual connection from their birth to death with universal electric energy continuum (cosmic consciousness). (c) Rebirth / reincarnation of individual souls, is scientifically impossible and continues to be a popular myth rather than a factual scientific truth. (d) Rebirth / reincarnation merely represents the birth of a new individual, resembling in its characteristics with someone who had lived in the historical past arising out of self-replicating behavior of the deoxyribonucleic acid (DNA) molecules in associated interaction with epigenetic environment which, in fact, is a modified version of the original electrical environment.

To sum up, this book is a *tour de force* and those who read it are sure to have an enriching experience. I congratulate Dr. Anil Moharir on this painstaking task and showing enough courage to back his scientific intuition and also for presenting a holistic multidisciplinary overview of the complex and socio-culturally controversial subjects of 'soul' and 'rebirth'. This is a splendid effort. For me, it had been a great pleasure and also a rewarding experience to read this book." --*Prof. Dr. Ravin L. Thatte, M.S. FRCS (Edin.)* *Plastic and Reconstructive Surgeon, Mumbai, Maharashtra, India*

"The book is an ambitious project by a scientist to decipher the concept of 'Soul', a mythical & mysterious entity invented by religious figures in all religions & invariably occurring in all religious discourses & scriptures. The author has read most of the latest literature on the subject but his emphasis is on correlating the concept as it occurs in religious and ancient texts, with the principles and relevant findings of modern science.

In doing so the author concludes that the Soul is nothing but electric charges flowing through the ion channels in all organisms. This reviewer would like to state that the electric charges have many attributes viz. handedness, speed, spin, magnetic moment, charge-charge interaction (e.g. electron- electron interaction), charge-lattice interaction (e.g. electron- phonon interaction, electron-magnon interaction), particle or wave nature of the charge & many more. Obviously if the electric charge is the de facto Soul then we have the possibilities of existence of countless numbers & types of souls. Is it acceptable to the men of science, scholars & common people.

An alternative to charge formalism would be the thermodynamics formalism. An organism is alive as long as it lives in an allowed energy regime dictated by the energy-budget regulated by various competing transport processes. If the physiological processes cannot function within the allowed/designated energy budget, the organism perishes. No need for soul here! *(My (Moharir's) conclusion from the discussion given in the book also points to this reality. An organism is alive as long as it retains its continued connection to the cosmic source of conscious potential energy (Electric Charge) and dies when that connection is severed by means of any dysfunction of its physiological, metabolic, regulated distribution and flow of electric charge by means of millions of ion-channels within bodies of living organisms)*

Another way of looking at the problem is by what can be called 'phase transition' formalism. Here there is a need to invoke the concept of the "order parameter" (op). The value of op is non-vanishing for a living organism & zero for the dead. In the complex system like an organism there will be enormous number of ops and one has to deal with coupled order parameters. Obviously, a soulless body has a zero value of order parameter."

This important book will serve as blue-print for further advancement in the subject of 'Soul'.

Dr. Dakshini Prasad Sharma, *Ex-Professor of Physics & Dean, Nagaland University, H Q Lumami, Nagaland, India.*

I am very sorry for the delay in sending my comments on your book "SOUL". My profound apologies!

Dr. Moharir, your book reflects your extra-ordinary intellectual abilities combined with communication expertise.

I have noted that you have rejected past and the current views that the soul, an imagined entity, is located lifelong in the body of an organism; instead you have proposed that the soul is actually a primal electric charge, not confined to the body, but which "remains in continual connection on its own with the universal consciousness (electric potential continuum) from the moment of conception, development, birth through its entire lifespan until its death by means of 'electrical charge' mediated through millions of ion channels in the bodies of living organisms". You have further argued that death in any multi-cellular organism is not an instantaneous process, but a gradual withdrawal of consciousness as a result of progressive closing of ion channels from various parts/organs in a sequential order.

While rejecting the concept of rebirth / reincarnation, you have argued, "rebirth/reincarnation merely represents the birth of a new individual, resembling in its characteristics with someone who had lived in the historical past arising out of the self-replicating behavior of the DNA molecules in associated interaction with epigenetic environment which, in fact, is a modified version of the original electrical environment.

You have indeed taken a broad, interdisciplinary canvas to draw and substantiate your viewpoints. You have succeeded in taking <u>an open-minded reader</u> to your viewpoint in part, if not in whole, which is a totally new and unique one. I find this book is dense and requires progression backwards and forwards through the pages of the book. This allows for a realistic sense of unpredictability, and leads to the possibility of repeat readings, which is one of the distinguishing features of the books. However, the author's viewpoint becomes clear.

The book sets up a new hypothesis, bordering on a theory, to explain the concept of soul. I should congratulate you for opening up a new direction to our thoughts on the concept of soul.

Whereas, I have no difficulty in accepting the view that an organism is born with a soul that actually is a primal electric charge, not confined to the body, but which "remains in continual connection on its own with the universal consciousness (electric potential continuum), and upon death merges with the "continuum". However, my mind does not easily reject the concept of rebirth/reincarnation.

It is believed by psychologists that memories are laid down as 'tracks' along certain axial neurons in the form of protein-glyphs, to which the name 'engram' has been given. Memory is the storage of these engrams, but the process of retrieving them is believed to be undertaken by a process called "ecphoriation: that has been described as: "The process whereby a representation of past experience is elicited." I wonder if we can formulate a conjecture that when a person dies suddenly, intact pieces of engrams are let loose in the electric potential continuum, and get lodged in the developing brain of a fetus at receptor sites. These pieces of engram become active at the right age of the developing organism. There are hundreds of records of children talking about the past life experiences. Could these be the engrams from a past generation?

I felt one lacuna while reading the book; absence of diagrams to show relationship and interactions. Such diagrams would help non-physicists like me to get quicker grasp of your written thought.

You have certainly added new ideas to the millennia-old debate on what is "soul".

Prof. Dr. Y. L. Nene, Retd. Deputy Director General, International Crop Research Institute for Semi-Arid and Tropics, (ICRISAT) Hyderabad, India and Chairman Emeritus-Asian Agri-History Foundation.
Dated January 27, 2018

Dear Anil,
I have completed first reading of your book on Soul, which is not sufficient to grasp everything you have so brilliantly stated. Your understanding of multiple disciplines of Science is astonishing and your attempt to intertwine them is laudable.

Soul remains as an enigma and future scientists hopefully will give us something we can digest and assimilate. My Marathi book on PUNARJANMA is expected to be published in April, where I have provided some 150 Indian/Foreigners' possibilities of Rebirth, for further exploration by all interested parties.

Surely, something or some part of a thing lives again. What we call it may not be more important than the thought and solace of the continuum of life. A human's current life is not the end of the story and even if very few people may appreciate this truth, our efforts may be worthwhile. I hope to meet you some time.

Best Regards,
Vidyadhar G. Oke

Dr. Vidyadhar G. Oke, *Thane, Maharashtra is a renowned Doctor of Medicine, besides an accomplished Harmonium Player, Musicologist, Musical Instrument Inventor and an Astrologer.*

Dear Moharir Saheb,
I am Dr. Shrikant Bhave from Baroda. Recently Mr. Vasant Pendharkar of your very old contact, presented me your book – "A Scientific Look At the Concept of Soul". I must congratulate you for your scholarly book on a subject which is of great interest of

research for several centuries. I am myself a student of yoga and esoteric science since last several decades but I find myself to be very primitive compared to you.

DR. SHRIKANT BHAVE
9824175099.
Shrikant Bhave srikantbhave4@gmail.com
March 31, 2018

Thank you very much. This looks like a marvelous book. Best Wishes,

Dean

Dean Radin, PhD
deanradin.org
- Chief Scientist, Institute of Noetic Sciences (IONS)
    noetic.org
- Distinguished Professor, Cal. Institute of Integral Studies
    ciis.edu
- President, Parapsychological Association
    parapsych.org
- Co-Editor-in-Chief, *Explore*, an Elsevier journal
    explorejournal.com
- Mailing address: IONS, 101 San Antonio Road, Petaluma, CA, 94952, USA

Summary statement on the contribution of the author Dr. A.V. Moharir to Science

Anil Vishnu Moharir (b. 1944 at Nagpur), holds Masters Degree in Physics from the Jiwaji University, Gwalior and Ph.D. from the Indian Institute of Technology, Delhi. Starting his research career from the National Physical Laboratory in 1967, he joined IARI-ICAR service in 1968 and served in various capacities as Senior Research Assistant, Scientist, Professor and Head, Division of Agricultural Physics. He initially worked on spectroscopic, spectro-photometric and electron microscopic studies of soils, plants and other biological materials and developed accurate spectro-photometric methods for trace determination of Iron and Titanium, many techniques for practical transmission electron microscopy and a new technique of Contact Electron Micrography for characterization of paper and thin film materials. Based on his studies on moisture hysteresis of seeds, he developed a simple laboratory procedure for screening drought tolerant wheat and rice varieties for cultivation under rainfed conditions and introduced a new concept of 'Normalized-Moisture-Hysteresis', which has found practical use in bakery and biscuit industry. Later he studied extensively the fine structure and structure-property relationships in native cotton fibres of varieties of all the four commercially cultivated species for helping cotton breeders in selecting parent genotypes for evolving new strains with inherent high fibre tenacity, as demanded by the modern Open-End-Rotor Spinning (OES) Technology. From X-Ray diffraction studies on bundles of cotton fibres, he identified cellulose crystallite orientation index (Hermans Crystallite Orientation Factor) to be the best index for characterization of cotton for tensile strength, both within individual species, within mixtures of *diploid* and *tetraploid* species and within a mixture of all species of cotton taken together. Prof. Moharir has published over one hundred twenty research papers in national and international journals, presented several at international conferences held in India, Germany, Belgium and USA as invited Keynote Speaker, translated and edited books, poems, religious discourses and texts from Hindi and Marathi into English. He served as Honorary Editor of the Indian Journal of Fibre and Textile Research (CSIR), Journal of Agricultural Research, Editor-in-Chief of the Journal of Agricultural Physics, as a regular referee for several other scientific journals, and as a Panel Scientist for the e-text book project of the National Institute of Science Communication (NISCOM-CSIR). A recipient of prestigious fellowships from the International Atomic Energy Agency, Vienna-Austria and the Commission of the European Communities, Brussels-Belgium, Prof. Moharir has successfully handled two international collaborative research projects on cotton. He has travelled extensively in England, Europe, Russia (USSR) and USA. Over half a dozen international biographical compilations on people of significant achievements have listed him for his contribution to science. Deeply interested in Hindustani classical vocal and instrumental music, Prof. Moharir is himself an accomplished portrait artist in charcoal medium and a connoisseur of fine art. After retirement from service in 2006, he is actively working for- 'Mission Health and Green India' besides regularly writing freelance on various scientific subjects from multi-disciplinary angles. His recent book- 'Profile in Solitude- Felicitation of Professor Atmaram Bhairav (A.B.) Joshi on his Ninety first Birthday with Foreword from Professor M. S. Swaminathan, Padma Vibhushan, FRS, FNI, FNAAS' is a *de-facto* national document on the life and contribution of Dr A B Joshi, the greatest agricultural scientist of the country to India's first Green Revolution. His other books- 'A Life of a Physicist in Agricultural Research' and 'Random Walks in Solitude-Essays in Multidisciplinary Explorations in Science' have been extolled as the unique and scholarly contributions to science by Padma Bhushan Professor Ram Badan Singh, President National Academy of Agricultural Sciences and by Professor Dr. Yeshwant L. Nene, Chairman, Asian Agri-History Foundation. Professor Moharir served as a member of the National Panel of Eminent Citizens of the Ministry of Rural Development, Government of India for evaluation of the projects executed under the Mahatma Gandhi National Rural Employment Guarantee Scheme (MGNREGA) in the state of Nagaland for over two years.

Other published books from the author;

1. 'ME MY OWN', English translation of 'Mee Maaza' book of short poems in Marathi by Chandrashekhar Gokhale. Translated into English by Anil Vishnu Moharir. Published by Mr. C.V. Garge, Managing Director, M/S Garud Travels, 1996.
2. 'Four Decades of Research in Agricultural Physics (ed.) Published by the Division of Agricultural Physics, Indian Agricultural Research Institute, New Delhi, 2003.
3. 'Profile in Solitude: Felicitation of Professor Atmaram Bhairav Joshi on his Ninety-First Birthday'. Felicitation Volume, A. V. Moharir (ed.) with Foreword by Padma Vibhushan Professor M.S. Swaminathan, FRS, FNI, FNAAS, Published by Mrs. Vimal Atmaram Joshi, 2007. **ISBN 978-81-7525-899-0.**
4. 'A Life of a Physicist in Agricultural Research', By Anil Vishnu Moharir, with Foreword by Padma Bhushan Professor Ram Badan Singh, President, National Academy of Agricultural Sciences, New Delhi. Published by the Author, 2013, pp 74. **ISBN 978-93-5126-183-4.**
5. 'Random Walks in Solitude: Essays in Multidisciplinary Explorations in Science' By Anil Vishnu Moharir, with Foreword by Dr. Yashwant L. Nene, Chairman Emeritus, Asian Agri-History Foundation, Secunderabad, Telangana. Published by the Author. 2013, pp 173. **ISBN 978-93-5137-154-0.**
6. A Scientific Look at the Concept of Soul : An Attempted Synthesis, By Anil Vishnu Moharir, with Foreword by Professor Dr. Ravin Lakshman Thatte, MS, FRCS (Edin.), ZORBA BOOKS, Gurugram, 2017, pp 118, **ISBN 978-93-5265-930-2.**

www.ingramcontent.com/pod-product-compliance
Lightning Source LLC
Chambersburg PA
CBHW062106080426
42734CB00012B/2775